TRUE STORIES OF NEW JERSEY

The First
Settler in
New Jersey

TRUE STORIES *of* NEW JERSEY

By

GRACE CROYLE HANKINS, B.S in Ed.

Daughter of the American Revolution
Daughter of Colonial Wars
Teacher, Woodrow Wilson Senior High School, Camden, N. J.

THE JOHN C. WINSTON COMPANY

CHICAGO   PHILADELPHIA   TORONTO
ATLANTA   SAN FRANCISCO   DALLAS

PRINTED IN THE U. S. A.
AT THE INTERNATIONAL PRESS
THE JOHN C. WINSTON CO., PROPRIETORS
PHILADELPHIA

DEDICATED TO
M. AND D.

FOR THE GREATER KNOWLEDGE
OF THE HISTORY OF
NEW JERSEY

PREFACE

The stories in this book are historic tales about our own state. They are stories of prominent persons, many of whose names are familiar to us; and of places in which many of us live or with which we are acquainted. The lives of these people in many ways were similar to our own. They went about their daily tasks, and experienced success or hardship in their efforts at gaining a livelihood very much as people do today. They dressed slightly differently years ago from the way people dress now. They walked or rode horseback or in wagons instead of in high-powered automobiles. But aside from such differences in living conditions, their lives were very much the same as ours are today.

New Jersey is the fourth smallest state in the United States, but it is far from being the fourth in historic lore. There are many good stories to be found in the history of the "Garden State." New Jersey had its Liberty Bell, its Tea Party, and even its "Paul Revere," although Hans Van Pelt's was a false alarm. One Jersey preacher gave hymn books to the soldiers for wadding for guns. A Jersey girl saved her pet horse by hiding him—you will never guess where!

As we travel over New Jersey, we find stories of Indians, pirates, brave soldiers and sailors, gallant leaders, famous people who did much to make our United States the great nation that it is today.

This book will tell you many of these stories of New Jersey. Some of them are given here exactly as the people told them themselves.

Several maps of different sections of the state will help you to locate the places that are mentioned in the text. The book is fully illustrated. As Alice said, "What is the use of a book without pictures?"

TABLE OF CONTENTS

(ix)

ACKNOWLEDGMENT

The author wishes to acknowledge the courtesy of the Pennsylvania Historical Society for permission to examine several first editions of New Jersey historical material. Acknowledgment is also due to A. Van Doren Honeyman, Editor of the Somerset County Historical Quarterly for "Middlebrook," by the Rev. Edward L. Jones, and "Hans Van Pelt," by Dr. Joseph Hunt Wilson; the American Book Company for "Grandfather's Rhyme" from *Stories of Great Americans for Little Americans*, by Edward Eggleston, 1895; the Board of Trustees of Old Tennent Church for quotations from the *Brochure on Old Tennent;* Rutgers University for condensed history of Rutgers and "On the Banks of the Old Raritan"; Charles D. Platt for "General Winds of Rockaway" and two stanzas of "The Winter Camp on the Wicke Farm" from *Ballads of New Jersey in the Revolution*, by C. D. Platt; Houghton, Mifflin Company for "The Village Blacksmith," by H. W. Longfellow; and "Caldwell of Springfield" from *Poetical Works of Bret Harte*, 1912; Reverend Doctor George Armstrong Liggett, of Springfield, for the poem "God's Acre"; Thomas Y. Crowell Company for "To a Locomotive," by Walt Whitman from *Leaves of Grass*.

LENNI-LENAPE

The first people in New Jersey were the Lenni-Lenape or Delaware Indians of the great family of the Algonquins. Their name means "first" or "original" people. It was these Indians that the Dutch and the Swedes found when they came to New Jersey.

They were friendly and peaceful. They were tall, well-built people with high cheek bones, copper-colored skin, and straight black hair. The men wore

THE ARROW MAKER
Bevan's Rock shelter group State Museum, Trenton.

(1)

scalp locks. They dressed in skins of wild animals, and painted their bodies with colors made from plant

Museum of the American Indian

DUGOUT DREDGED UP IN THE HACKENSACK RIVER

juices and clay. They painted their faces in different colors to express different emotions.

The Lenni-Lenape lived in huts made of stout saplings or young trees bent to form a shelter and then covered with bark, grasses, or clay.

The women built the huts, prepared the meals, and made the clothing from the skins of animals. They also made ornaments from clay and shells. To make bread, they ground corn in a stone mortar with a pestle, and made the bread from the coarse meal thus prepared.

The men hunted, fished, and fought. They made their hatchets and arrowheads of flint and quartz. They made crude canoes by burning out the center of tree trunks with fire, and chipping away the charred part with their stone tools.

Their food consisted of maize or Indian corn, beans, wild turkey, fish, and the flesh of wild animals. The Indians of New Jersey also knew shellfish, such as oysters, clams, and crabs. All these they used as food.

In 1758, seeing that in a short time the Indians would no longer have any land to live on, the government set aside the first Indian Reservation in what is now the United States, at Indian Mills, Burlington

County, New Jersey. At the time of the Revolution, all the Lenni-Lenapes' land had been sold to the white settlers.

Soon, in their greed for land, the white men took away this Reservation and moved the Indians to New York State, from there to Green Bay, Wisconsin, and finally to Indian Territory, Oklahoma. So that, today, you may find a Lenni-Lenape, whose fathers hunted on the mighty

Museum of the American Indian

STONE MORTAR AND PESTLE FOR GRINDING CORN

Delaware, far from his native hunting grounds. As evidence of the two thousand red men that once roamed New Jersey, there now remain pottery jars, beads, arrowheads, bones dug up on the sites of once busy Indian villages, and Indian names of streams and places that once belonged to the Lenni-Lenapes.

THE FIRST SCHOOL

The first school in New Jersey was opened in the village of Bergen in 1662. Engelbert Stuynhuysen was the first schoolmaster. It was part of his job to find a convenient place to keep school.

The early schools were very different from ours. The schoolhouses were built of logs and clay with dirt floors. They had rough wooden benches for seats. Logs, burned in the fireplace, heated the room.

THE FIRST SCHOOL PROBABLY LOOKED LIKE THIS

The schoolbooks were few and uninteresting. The little children learned their lessons from a hornbook. It was not really a book but a piece of paper with printing on it. This paper was fastened to a flat piece of wood and covered with transparent horn.

Goose-quill pens were used in writing. The teachers made and mended the pens. This was no easy task. There was little taught except reading, writing, and ciphering (arithmetic).

All the grades were in one room and there was only one teacher. When a class was "called," the children

in that class took their books to the front of the room
and the teacher "heard the lesson."

If a child did not know his lesson, he was made to
sit on a high stool in the front of the room and wear
a dunce's cap, a tall, pointed, paper cone.   If a pupil
was disobedient, he was beaten with the ferule, or with
a birchrod.

Here is a "want-ad" that was printed in the
Weekly Post Boy, of March 23, 1747:

> "A good schoolmaster for children, one who can
> teach reading, writing, and ciphering, at Rariton,
> about six miles above Bound Brook.   Any person
> properly qualified may meet with good encourage-
> ment by apply to
>
> John Broughton."

PINE LIGHTS

In early days, the colonist had to supply nearly all
his own needs.   He built the house, made the furniture, built the barns, farmed the fields, cared for the
livestock.   He had to provide food for himself and
family; he raised sheep to supply wool which his
wife combed, carded, spun, dyed, wove into cloth, and
made into garments for the family.   He, also, frequently raised flax which was manufactured into
linen cloth in his home.   His wife braided rugs, made
the clothing, cooked the food, made soap and candles,
and helped her husband with the chores on the farm.

Farmers and their wives in distant parts of the country still perform many of these tasks for themselves,

2

but there is one job, in particular, that has disappeared: the making of lights.

The people in New Jersey, as in all the colonies, made use of the materials they had at hand: tallow, from sheep or cattle, was made into candles by using candle molds or simply by dipping a cord repeatedly into the melted tallow until it took on the size and shape of a candle. Sometimes the supply of candles became exhausted; then the colonist brought pine knots from the woods, and burned these for light in his home.

Pine knots from trees of Pitch Pine or Torch Pine made, perhaps, the best lights. The leaves of these trees are from three to five inches long, and grow in bundles of three. The cones are egg-shaped, one, two, or three and a half inches long; sometimes they are found in clusters. The bark is reddish brown to black and thickens early in the life of the trees. These trees sometimes grow to a height of seventy feet, and often are two and one-half feet in diameter. They are the most fire-resistant evergreens in eastern North America. They burn slowly, and are ideal for use as a light.

Torch Pine is so-called because of the fact that the early settlers used it not only for lighting their cabins but for light when traveling at night.

R. Tait McKenzie

FRANKLIN AT THE AGE OF 17 WHEN HE ARRIVED IN PHILADELPHIA

AN EARLY VISITOR

When Benjamin Franklin left Boston, in 1723, looking for work, he went first to New York. Meeting with no success there, he decided to go to Philadelphia.

He went by boat from New York to Amboy and then began his long journey on foot across New Jersey to Burlington. From there he hoped to get a sailboat going down the river to Philadelphia.

Shortly after he started, it began to rain; he soon was wet to the skin and splashed all over with the red mud of central New Jersey. But he kept on. He spent one night at Doctor Brown's Tavern at the corner of Crosswicks Avenue and Farnsworth Street in Bordentown, where Ye Olde Washington House stands today. (You can follow his path on the map.)

At Bordentown, he took a passage with some others in a rowboat. They were delayed coming down the river and by the time they arrived near where they thought Philadelphia was, it was dark. In those days there were no street lights in Philadelphia and the colonists went to bed early. Fearing, because of the darkness, that they might possibly pass their destination, they disembarked on the nearest bank of the Delaware—the New Jersey side of the river—and camped on the banks of a small stream for the night. That small stream was Cooper's Creek. The spot where they camped is now in the city of Camden.

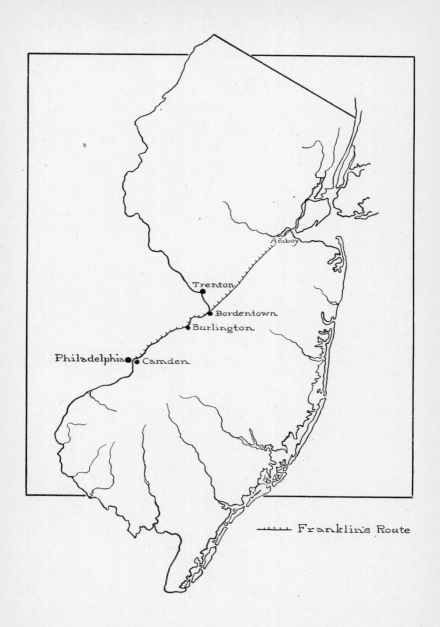

Franklin's Route

The next morning they found that they had camped directly across the river from their destination. They rowed across and arrived in Philadelphia on Sunday morning.

The journey from New York to Philadelphia had taken six days. Today, it can be done in less than two hours by train, and approximately one hour by airplane.

Later, when Franklin became a great man, he frequently took drives through what is now Camden County. It is said to have been his favorite pastime.

COLONIAL PETS

Upon trial it has been found that the following animals and birds which are wild in the woods of North America can be made nearly as tame as domestic animals. The calves of the wild cows (bison) which are found in Carolina, and other provinces to the south of Pennsylvania, can be brought up among tame cattle. When they are grown up they are perfectly tame but at the same time very unruly, so that no enclosure is strong enough to resist them if they had a mind to break through it. As they possess great strength in their necks it is easy for them to overthrow the fences with their horns, and to get into the cornfields.

The American deer can likewise be tamed, and I have seen them tame myself in several different places. A farmer in New Jersey had one in his possession, which he caught when it was very young; at present, it is so tame that in the daytime it runs into

SOME OF THE GAME BIRDS AND ANIMALS OF NEW JERSEY

the woods for its food, and toward night returns home, frequently bringing a wild deer out of the woods, giving its master an opportunity to shoot it at his very door.

Beavers have been tamed to such an extent that they have brought home what they caught by fishing to their masters. This is often the case with otters, of which I have seen some that were as tame as dogs, and followed their master wherever he went; if he went out in a boat the otter went with him, jumped into the water and after a while came up with a fish.

The raccoon can in time be made so tame as to run about the streets like a domestic animal; but it is impossible to make it leave off its habit of stealing. In the dark it creeps to the poultry, and kills a whole flock in one night. Sugar and other sweet things must be carefully hidden from it; for if the chests and boxes are not always locked, it gets into them and eats the sugar and licks up the molasses with its paws. The ladies, therefore, have some complaint against it.

The gray and flying squirrels are so tamed by the boys that they sit on their shoulders and follow them everywhere.

The turkey cocks and hens run about in the woods of this country and differ in no respect from our tame ones, except in their superior size and more palatable flesh. When their eggs are found in the woods and put under tame turkey hens, the young ones become tame; however, when they grow up, it sometimes happens that they fly away; their wings are therefore commonly clipped especially when they are young.

Wild geese have, likewise, been tamed in the following manner. When the wild geese first come hither in the spring and stop a little while the people try to shoot them in the wing. They then row to the place where the wild goose fell, catch it and keep it for some time at home; by this means many of them have been made so tame that when they were let out in the morning they returned in the evening; but to be more sure of them, their wings are commonly clipped.

Partridges which are here in abundance, can be so far tamed as to run about all day with the poultry, coming along with them to be fed, when they are called. In the same manner I have seen wild pigeons so tame that they will fly out and return again.

—PETER KALM (1748)

From: *Travels in North America*, by Peter Kalm, Professor of Oeconomy in the University of Aobo in Swedish Finland, and Member of the Swedish Royal Academy of Sciences, Translated into English by John Reinhold Forster, F.A.S. Printed by William Eyres, Warrington, 1770. Vol. I, 207–210.

MOSQUITO FORT

When they swat a mosquito, few people think that they are striking one reason why we speak English in New Jersey instead of Swedish.

When this country was all wilderness, it seemed to the Europeans to offer many ways to "get rich quick." Every country wanted colonies in the New World.

It so happened that the Swedes and the Holland Dutch selected the land along the Delaware River for settlement at about the same time. First, the Dutch would build a fort to protect their colonists and to

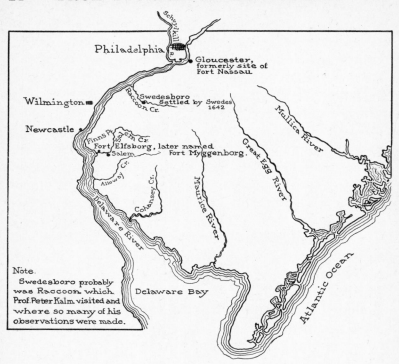

promote trade to enrich Holland; then, the Swedes would build a fort not far away to protect their colonists and to promote Swedish trade as well as to hinder the Dutch as much as possible.

When, about 1623, the Dutch built Fort Nassau, near where Gloucester City now is, the first European settlement on the Delaware River, the Swedes built Fort Elfsborg on Salem Creek. From Fort Elfsborg, the Swedish ships were saluted as they passed, and Dutch ships were compelled to lower their flags.

Here, our little friend took part in the contest. There are numerous swamps near Salem Creek, as there are along many creeks in southern New Jersey. The mosquitoes breed rapidly in such places. Now, mosquitoes seem to relish a chance to feed on a blond complexioned person, much more than on a dark person. Perhaps, because a blond person's skin is thinner and more "tender." How delighted all these "skeeters" must have been to have the Swedes, who are mostly blonds, settle so near the breeding grounds, after so many years of having only the dark skinned Indians to feed upon. The Swedish settlers truly must have seemed a banquet to the ever-hungry mosquitoes.

While the mosquitoes were pleased, needless to say the Swedes were not. What with the mosquitoes and the Dutch fighting them, the Swedes became disgusted. They abandoned and destroyed Fort Elfsborg which had earned the name of Fort Myggenborg or Mosquito (Myggor) Fort, and finally gave up their colonies. Later, the Dutch ceded New Jersey, which was part of New Netherlands, to the English.

A hundred years later, the mosquitoes were still to be reckoned with according to the famous Swedish traveler and naturalist, Professor Peter Kalm.

Today, many of these salt marshes which breed mosquitoes have been drained, but, even so, it is possible to appreciate Peter Kalm's wonder at the "blisters" as he called the mosquito bites.

ABOUT BEARS AND MOSQUITOES

Bears are very numerous up in the country and do much mischief. Mr. Bartram told me, that when a bear catches a cow, he kills her in the following manner.

He bites a hole into the hide, and blows with all his power into it, till the animal swells excessively and dies; for the air expands greatly between the flesh and the hide.

An old Swede, called Nils Gustave's son, who was ninety-one years of age, said that in his youth, the bears had been very frequent hereabouts, but that they had seldom attacked the cattle: that whenever a bear was killed, its flesh was prepared like pork, and it had a very good taste.

The flesh of bears is still prepared like ham, on the River Morris (Maurice River) in New Jersey. The environs of Philadelphia, and even the whole province of Pennsylvania in general contain very few bears, for they have been extirpated by degrees. In Virginia, they kill them in several different ways. Their flesh is eaten by rich and poor, since it is reckoned equal in goodness to pork. In some parts of this province where no hogs can be kept on account of the great numbers of bears, the people are used to catch and kill them, and to use them instead of hogs. The American bears, however, are said to be less fierce and dangerous than the European ones.

The gnats, which are very troublesome at night here, are called *mosquetoes*. They are exactly like the gnats in Sweden, only somewhat smaller in size. In daytime or at night they come into the houses and when the people are gone to bed they begin their disagreeable humming, approach always nearer to the bed, and at last suck up so much blood that they can hardly fly away. Their bite causes blisters on people of a delicate complexion.

When the weather has been cool for some days, the mosquitoes disappear. But when it changes again, and especially after the rain, they gather frequently in such quantities about the houses that their numbers are astonishing. The chimneys of the English, which have no valves for shutting them up afford the gnats a free entrance into the houses. In sultry evenings, the mosquitoes accompany the cattle in great swarms from the woods to the houses, or to town, and when the cattle are driven past the houses the gnats fly in wherever they can.

In the greatest heat of the summer they are so numerous in some places, that the air seems to be quite full of them, especially near swamps and stagnant water, such as the River Morris (Maurice) in New Jersey. The inhabitants, therefore, make a big fire before their houses to expel these disagreeable guests by the smoke. The old Swedes here said that gnats had formerly been much more numerous; that even at present they swarmed in vast quantities on the seashore near the salt water; and that those which troubled us this autumn in Philadelphia were of a more poisonous kind than they commonly used to be. This last quality appeared from the blisters which were formed on the spots where the gnats had made their sting. In Sweden, I never felt any other inconvenience from their sting than a little itching where they sucked. But when they stung me, here, at night, my face was so disfigured by little red spots and blisters that I was almost ashamed to show myself.

—PETER KALM (1748)

A

LETTER

FROM

NEW JERSEY,

IN

AMERICA,

GIVING SOME

ACCOUNT and DESCRIPTION

OF THAT

PROVINCE.

By a GENTLEMAN, late of
CHRIST'S College, CAMBRIDGE.

The rev.^d Mr. Thomas Thompson A.M

LONDON:

Printed for M. COOPER in Pater-noster-row.
M.DCC.LVI.

IN NEW JERSEY

The —————— province of New Jersey, which I come now to give you some description of, has been settled a little above a hundred years. It is as well cultivated as any of the colonies, yet is much in dishabille, or at least seems so, to one that has not seen late settled places. The farms which lye interspersed in the bottom of thick woods, resemble the face of the sky after a tempest, when the clouds are breaking away and dispersing.

The pleasantest spots that you see here are but homely beauties; and one finds none of those landscapes which our island of Great Britain affords. Almost, wherever you pass upon the roads, you are either in woods, or have woods on one side of you; and the view which is on the open side is terminated —————— within the breadth of a field or two, so that the horizon is hardly any where clear, and to view the country from an eminence, it seems to be almost all woods.

The roads in most places are very good, but then you travel in a maze, having neither mile-stone, nor Mercury for your direction; only here and there is a tree marked with the initial letter of the name of the next town, but so ill cut, that one can hardly know it to be an alphabetical character.

A few scattered houses make here a village; and in those towns where the buildings stand in line, they are not contiguous. Most of the houses are wooden structures, compiled of pine boards or cedar shingles.

*   *   *   *   *   *   *   *

The people are naturally brisk, and of a lively temper. They stand much upon a footing of equality among each other, and those of the common sort, by conversing freely with persons in office and commission, acquire a knowledge of things and business, and receive a brightening, by which they are far superior to our countrymen of the same rank.

Religion is here divided into many sects and parties; and the men, who are extreme kind husbands, go commonly the way that the wife is of.

*   *   *   *   *   *   *   *

The poor people in general live better here than, I believe, most where, by the favour of the plenty and cheapness of provisions; besides, getting their children into good families by the time they are six or seven years of age, they have little experience of the charge of them, so that very few turn beggars, or go to seek their bread from home, but with their working tools upon their backs.

You must certainly think, that thefts and robberies cannot but be very rife among us, as these colonies are obliged to take all the rogues and villains that are yearly transported from the several jails in England. But I can assure you, it is far otherwise; and people think so little of the danger of these things, that many families never fasten their doors when they go to bed; and the good housewives that have cloth in bleaching, never take it in at nights. As to picking of pockets, the practice is utterly unknown, and the roads are perfectly uninfested and secure.

But the wonder of this will evaporate, when I tell you that none of the Newgate gentry are landed here,

SOUTH JERSEY APPLE BLOSSOMS

but always either in Virginia, or some of the southern
colonies, where, however, they are no calamity: for
the masters of the transports make them all bind
themselves by indenture to him for four years,—and
they are obliged to honest labor.

The spring is here commonly late, but when the year
does begin to dress, the ornaments of nature are out
all at once.   In a few days the scene is quite changed.
The vast orchards are clad in a thick bloom, which
makes the country look and smell like paradise. . . .

The country is well watered with fine streams and
rivers, and every house has a draw-well.

The woods, although abounding with very beautiful
birds, are the dullest of all sylvan scenes.   The
mocking bird is the mimick of them all, and a complete
droll in his way. . . . But nothing is so beautiful and
diminutive, as that little feathered spark, the humming
bird, who with the most gallant address courts the
daughters of the garden in a coat of plumage composed
of the finest feathers.

*   *   *   *   *   *   *   *

In summer time, for about two months, the air is
bespangled every night with a kind of flies which they
call fireflies.   They are very much in swamps and
woods of a wet soil, and in those gloomy places make
an extraordinary appearance.   Their light is not
steady;—and in the silent night, hovering about in
their bright form, they almost give the mind an
impression of being haunted there.

—BY A GENTLEMAN (1745–1755)

SALEM OAK

Old Salem Oak, in Friends Cemetery, Salem, New Jersey.

Height, 73 feet.

Trunk, 30 feet, 5 inches in circumference at largest part; five feet from ground, 19 feet.

Covers about 10,156 square feet, or about one quarter of an acre.

Age, over 500 years old.

Measurements certified by James S. Sparks, Civil Engineer, March 11, 1933.

During the past ten years $2,000 has been spent on this tree for expert tree surgery and attention.

Under this tree, legend says, John Fenwick who was granted a large part of southern New Jersey, made a treaty with the Indians in 1675, giving 4 guns and lead, 10½ ankers of rum (about 336 gallons), some shirts, shoes and stockings, 4 blankets, 16 matched coats, 1 piece of matched coating and other English goods.

Seedlings from the Old Oak have been planted from coast to coast. A very fine tree is now growing in William Luna Park, Sacramento, California.

All acorns are gathered by the Society of Friends each year. Nurserymen and Park Commissioners have standing orders for the acorns before they fall. Owing to the age of the tree some seasons there are very few acorns.

This famous tree, a survivor of the original forest, is still standing on West Broadway facing Oak Street in Salem.

Courtesy Esso Tours and William W. Klenke

HANCOCK HOUSE NEAR SALEM, BUILT 1734

MASSACRE AT HANCOCK'S BRIDGE

Salem Celebrates June 16, 1934

News Item

The two hundredth anniversary of the old Hancock House at Salem, New Jersey, will be celebrated on June 16. It will be attended by the governor and by representatives of State historical societies. Restored in 1932 by the Salem County Historical Society, the house is now a museum.

When you drive out, notice the skilful use of blue glazed brick for decoration in the walls. On one end of the house the builder's initials and the date — 1734 — have been worked into the bricks—sure proof of the age of this landmark.

The interior has hand-carved paneling and finish, unexpected in a farmhouse built in 1734. Many original panes of glass have escaped the stones of mischievous small boys for two hundred years. All of the furnishings are either authentic antiques or perfect reproductions.

Probably the things which will hold your interest longest in Hancock House are the household and farming tools used long before the Revolution, and such objects as primitive animal traps and ox yokes. On a fine old four-poster bed is a patchwork quilt that will make the ladies of your party a bit envious. The four-poster has its trundle bed to match.

In the attic you can see sinister stains beneath the eaves where a party of Continentals was massacred in 1778. It is claimed to be the only house still standing in which a Revolutionary massacre actually took place.

Behind it is a "plank house," also restored, which antedates the Hancock House by many years. Apparently it was built by a shipwright, as each plank is so perfectly fitted to the next. It is built of white cedar, four inches thick, impossible to duplicate now.

—From *Esso Tours*

THE GREENWICH TEA BURNING

Many of the taxes that the American colonists were forced to pay were objectionable to them, but none more than the tax on tea. The colonists resisted the enforcement of the payment of this tax in a public outburst at Boston in 1773, which is known as the *Boston Tea Party*.

People, everywhere, refused to buy English tea and the London merchants were worried. The East India Company had seventeen million pounds of tea in its

warehouses ready to be shipped to America. They
tried various ways of getting the tea into the colonies
thinking that,
if it could once
be landed and
put on sale, the
American tea
drinkers would
gladly buy it.

The ship,
Greyhound,
loaded with
tea, sailed up
the Delaware
River toward
Philadelphia.
The captain
was afraid to
go to Philadel-
phia because,

HOUSE IN WHICH THE TEA WAS STORED,
GREENWICH

from that port, tea-ships were sent back to England as
soon as they arrived. Instead, on November 22, 1774,
he put into Cohansey Creek, and anchored at the little
town of Greenwich. He figured that he could land his
tea at Greenwich and, that from there, the tea could
be taken to the dealers and sold.

He felt he was very clever to have succeeded in
landing his cargo safely. But little did he know the
independent Jerseymen.

The citizens of Greenwich had been too few to
resist the landing of the tea. But they did not like
the idea of having their little village used by the

tea merchants to force taxed tea down their neighbors throats.

The patriotic citizens gathered together and resolved that, though the tea was already in their town, it should not go out. They would show the British tyrant that Cohansey Creek was no safer than Boston Harbor for the detestable tea.

A party of forty young men was organized to destroy the tea. They dressed as Indians in order to disguise themselves, and to frighten intruders.

They gathered in the market place, rushed the house where the tea was stored, broke open the doors, carried out the tea, split open the boxes in which it was contained, and made a great pile of it. Lighting the dry tea, they soon had a magnificent bonfire. And there was no one who even attempted to put it out.

WHARF WHERE SHIP *GREYHOUND* LANDED TEA DESTROYED
AT GREENWICH

THE GREENWICH TEA PARTY

Can you picture the feelings of the British captain when he found the tea, so safely stored away, destroyed?

MONUMENT TO COMMEMORATE
THE GREENWICH TEA BURNING

He was angry and when he learned the men's names who took part in the tea burning, he sued them for the damage done his property. It was not difficult to learn the names of the "Indians" because they were proud of what they had done and boasted of it. Among this patriotic band were: Dr. Ebenezer Hunt; Richard Howell, a young law student, afterwards a Major in the Army and Governor of New Jersey; David Pierson; Stephen Pierson; Silas Whitacar; Timothy Elmer; Rev. Andrew Hunter; Rev. Philip Fithian; Alexander Moore, Jr.; Clarence Parvin; John Hunt; James Hunt; Lewis Howell; Henry Stacks; James Ewing; Dr. Thomas Ewing; Josiah Seeley; and Joel Fithian.

Their friends and neighbors were, also, proud of them and prepared to help them. They collected money to hire lawyers to defend them. The lawyers for the "Indians" were General Joseph Bloomfield, Elias Boudinot, Jonathan Dickinson, Sergeant and George Read.

When the case came before the Grand Jury, the judge ordered the jury to indict the tea-burners; but the jury refused to do so.   How the case would have ended, we have no way of knowing because the War of the Revolution began and the case was dropped. We may draw our own conclusions, however, for today a monument marks the site of the Greenwich Tea Burning and on it are inscribed the names of the "Indians."

NEW JERSEY'S LIBERTY BELL

While the world famous Liberty Bell hangs in Independence Hall, Philadelphia, just a few miles south of Philadelphia, across the Delaware River, is New Jersey's own Liberty Bell.

When the news that independence was declared; that the colonies were now the United States of America; that the colonists were no longer British subjects, but free and independent citizens, the bell in the tower of Cumberland County's first brick courthouse at Cohansey Bridge, now Bridgeton,

clanged out the tidings to the Jersey men and women of the surrounding countryside.

It had been bought by their contributions and cast in Bridgewater, Massachusetts, in 1763.

It remained in the Courthouse Tower until 1846,

NEW JERSEY LIBERTY BELL

(32)

when the old building was torn down.   It was then transferred to Fireman's Hall and served for nine years as a fire alarm;   then it was removed to the cupola on the West Jersey Academy;   still later, we find it at the Bridgeton High School, Broad and Lawrence Streets.   Now, after nearly two hundred years of service, it reposes in a room given over to historic relics at the Bridgeton Courthouse, where you can see it on Wednesday afternoons.

Bridgeton is situated on the Cohansey Creek, northeast of Greenwich.

THIS MARKER IS IN FRONT OF THE BRIDGETON HIGH SCHOOL

WHERE SATURDAY IS SUNDAY IN NEW JERSEY

There is a quaint little story told of the naming of Shiloh near Bridgeton in Cumberland County.

The town was first settled in 1705 by Robert Ayres, a Seventh Day Baptist.   The followers of this belief celebrate Saturday as the Seventh Day or the Day of Rest, rather than Sunday as many religions do.   They go to church on Saturday and work on Sunday.

Robert Ayres purchased two thousand acres of land at Cohansey Corners which he sold to the people of his own faith in order that they might have a town of their own and keep the Seventh Day as they wished.

There was a log church there which the people desired to move. In the moving, it got stuck at a point where six roads meet. Ayres announced that the "Ark of the Lord (that is the church) rested at Shiloh" and Cohansey Corners accordingly became known as Shiloh and is so known to this day.

A SOLDIER OF OLD GLOUCESTER

The almost miraculous escape of Miles Sage forms the favorite theme of every Old Gloucester soldier. Miles was in the dragoon service, and a braver trooper never lived.

On one occasion, while Haddonfield was occupied by Ellis' regiment, to which our hero belonged, he, in company with one Ben Haines, was ordered to reconnoitre the enemy, who lay near Gloucester Point.

Sage, having lost his companion, reached the Point and learned that the British had already moved for Haddonfield, intending a surprise upon the Americans. He turned his fleet and faithful mare, and dashed off through the darkness of the night, for the camp.

Driving on through Newton Creek, and over ditches and hedges with the speed of the wind, he reached the village and stopped before Colonel Ellis' quarters to give the alarm. It was needless, for the house was already filled with British officers.

He mounted again without having been discovered, and galloped off to find his retreating countrymen. Near the eastern extremity of the town, the enemy

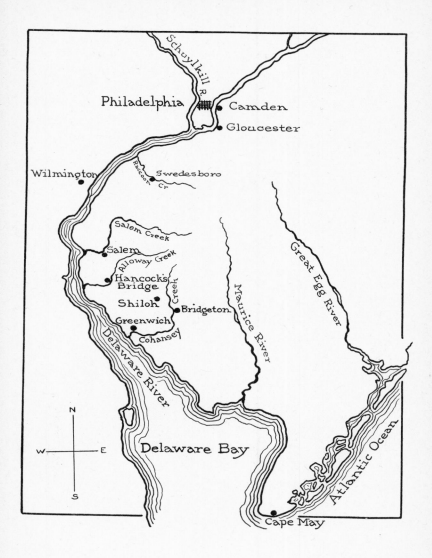

was drawn up in three ranks. Through two ranks the trooper charged successfully; but at the third his mare fell, and left him at the mercy of his foes.

They surrounded him, and pierced him with no less than thirteen bayonet wounds! A Scotch officer here interposed, and had him carried to the village inn, where he was put under the care of some women.

One of these beseeching him to remember heaven, he exclaimed, "Why Martha, I mean to give the enemy thirteen rounds yet."

He lived to tell his grandchildren of his fearful adventure, and we have no doubt, to remember heaven too.

Isaac Mickle (1845)
Reminiscence of Old Gloucester

WASHINGTON'S LAST VISIT TO
NEW JERSEY

Up the road leading from Cooper's Ferry (now Camden), the great and good Washington used to ride, when President, to muse upon the eventful scenes through which he had passed, and to breathe, perhaps, in solitude his grateful acknowledgments to God for his country's salvation.

The last time President Washington took his accustomed ride upon this road—early in 1797—a Hessian who had deserted at the battle of Trenton, named Harry Dheets, chanced to meet him near the ferry.

"We were unloading some wood near the ferry," says our informant, a worthy old gentleman yet resident in Camden (1845), "when Washington, entirely unattended, rode slowly past. I knew him, and bowed, as did the Hessian also. Washington returned the acknowledgment with his accustomed politeness, and was passing on, when Dheets addressed him:

"'I tink I has seen your face before—vat ish your name?'

"The General drew up his beautiful gray, and bowing to the man, replied, 'My name is George Washington.'

"Half frightened out of his wits, the poor Dutchman exclaimed, 'Oh, mine Gott! I vish I vas unter te ice—I vish I vas unter te ice!'

"Washington kindly assured him that he had done no harm—rode a short distance up the road to the

4   (37)

WASHINGTON GREETS THE HESSIAN

row of mulberry trees which you doubtless remember—and sat there some time in his saddle, looking over the remains of the works which the British army had thrown up during the war.   He, then, turned his horse, rode slowly past us again, and crossed the river."

This is the last time he ever visited New Jersey, as he retired to Mount Vernon soon afterwards.

ISAAC MICKLE (1845)
Reminiscence of Old Gloucester

THE KING CITY—BORDENTOWN

Did you know that Bordentown got its name, the King City, from the fact that a King of Spain once lived there?

When Napoleon Bonaparte was defeated at the Battle of Waterloo, all his friends and relatives were forced to run for their lives.

His brother, Joseph Bonaparte, whom Napoleon had made King of Spain, was forced to flee to America. He came to Bordentown, New Jersey in 1815.

Here, he purchased a country estate, Point Breeze Park, on Park Street, and lived there under the title of Comte de Survilliers. Congress passed a special law enabling him, as an alien, to own land in this country.

He was hospitable, kind, and agreeable. He entertained many distinguished visitors, among whom was General Lafayette.

He left America in 1832 but returned for two more years in 1837.

From King Joseph's residence here, New Jersey received its nickname "Spain" and Bordentown, its name "King City."

CLARA BARTON'S SCHOOL

The name of Clara Barton is known far and wide as the founder of the American Red Cross. It is an honored name. Much good has come of this woman's desire to help suffering human beings.

But one thing Clara Barton did, which means so much to the children of New Jersey, was to found the first free public school in the state, in Bordentown, in 1853.

Miss Barton was born in Oxford, Massachusetts, on Christmas Day in 1821. She received her education at Clinton Liberal Institute in Clinton, New York. She was teaching at Hightstown, New Jersey, when she learned of the great need for a free school in Bordentown.

In those days, if the parents could not afford a private teacher or could not afford to send their son or

Courtesy of the Red Cross
CLARA BARTON

daughter to a private school—the child simply got no education. Can you think what it would mean to you not to be able to write your own name or to read anything at all? More boys than girls went to school because, as a general thing, educating girls was thought to be a waste of time and money.

In 1853, Miss Barton went to Bordentown and opened the first free public school in New Jersey in an old building which had been used for a school for many years. This building stands at the intersection of Crosswicks and Burlington streets.

She taught in Bordentown from 1853 to 1854, a little more than a year, when because of ill health she had to give up her beloved teaching. From 1854 to 1857 she worked in the Patent Office at Washington, D. C. When the Civil War broke out she took up the work which grew into the American Red Cross.

CLARA BARTON'S SCHOOLHOUSE AT BORDENTOWN

The Clara Barton Schoolhouse, at Bordentown, was neglected for many years. In 1920, pupils and teachers in the public schools of New Jersey and others interested in restoring the schoolhouse so that it might be preserved as a memorial to that famous woman, contributed money for that purpose. The property was owned by Thomas J. Rattigan, who lived until recently next door to the school, and who generously donated the site.

On Saturday, June 11, 1921, the building was dedicated with impressive ceremonies. Two of Clara Barton's relatives were present: Stephen Barton, her nephew; and Miss Saidee F. Riccius, her grand-niece. There were also present representatives of the state and county governments.

Clara Barton gave a great gift to all humanity when she founded the American Red Cross; she gave a very special gift to New Jersey when she founded its first free public school.

JOHN WOOLMAN, THE FRIEND OF THE SLAVES

John Woolman was a Friend or Quaker who lived in Mount Holly, New Jersey, on the road to Springfield. His writings are still respected highly all over the world as the work of a good and wise man. His "Journal" or diary is included by Doctor Eliot in his "Five Foot Shelf of Books." He worked untiringly against slavery, being one of the first workers against slavery in this country.

He is described by John Greenleaf Whittier as being "only four and a half feet high, hunch-backed, with projecting chest, legs small and uneven, arms longer than his legs; a huge head, showing only, beneath the enormous white hat, large, solemn eyes, and a prominent nose; the rest of his face covered with a snowy semicircle of beard falling low on his breast— a figure to recall the old legends of a—brownie."

He was frequently asked as a respected member of the community to draw up wills. He tells of one such occasion in his "Journal" for the year 1755.

"Scrupling to do writings (wills) relative to keeping slaves has been a means of sundry small trials to me, in which I have so evidently felt my own will set aside that I think it good to mention a few of them. Tradesmen and retailers of goods, who depend on their business for a living, are naturally inclined to keep the good will of their customers [he was a tailor

JOHN WOOLMAN'S HOUSE, MOUNT HOLLY

by trade]; nor is it a pleasant thing for young men to be under any necessity to question the judgment or honesty of elderly men, and more especially of such as have a fair reputation. Deep-rooted customs, though wrong, are not easily altered; but it is the duty of all to be firm in that which they certainly know is right for them.

"A charitable benevolent man, well acquainted with a Negro, may, I believe, under some circumstances, keep him in his family as a servant, on no other motives than the Negro's good, but man, as man, knows not what shall be after him, nor hath he any assurance that his children will attain to that perfection in wisdom and goodness necessary rightly to exercise such power: hence it is clear to me, that I ought not to be the scribe where wills are drawn in which some children are made—masters over others during life.

"About this time an ancient man of good esteem in the neighborhood came to my house to get his will written. He had young Negroes, and I asked him privately how he purposed to dispose of them. He told me; I then said, 'I cannot write thy will without breaking my own peace,' and respectfully gave him my reasons for it. He signified that he had a choice that I should have written it, but as I could not, consistently with my conscience, he did not desire it, and so he got it written by some other person. A few years after, there being great alterations in his family, he came again to get me to write his will. His Negroes were yet young, and his son, to whom he intended to give them, was, since he first spoke to me, from a libertine become a sober young man, and he supposed that I would have been free on that account to write it. We had much friendly talk on the subject, and then deferred it. A few days after he came again and directed their freedom, and then I wrote his will."

You can visit John Woolman's house, today, in Mount Holly, and, if the weather permits, have tea in his yard.

Quotations from *John Woolman's Journal* with an introduction by J. G. Whittier, Published by J. R. Osgood & Company, Boston, 1873.

NEW JERSEY'S SIGNERS

New Jersey elected five delegates to the Second Continental Congress which drew up the Declaration of Independence. Each of these five men signed this famous document.

SIGNATURES OF NEW JERSEY SIGNERS
OF THE DECLARATION OF INDEPENDENCE

They were:
Richard Stockton: son of John; great-grandson of Richard, who came from England to Long Island before 1670 and about 1680 purchased 6,400 acres at Princeton, N. J.; born near Princeton, October 1, 1730; graduated at Princeton, 1748; admitted to the bar, 1754; member of Council, 1768; justice of the Supreme Court, 1774; elected to Congress, 1776; prisoner of war; died in Princeton, February 28, 1781.

John Witherspoon: born in Scotland, 1723; minister of the Gospel; president of Princeton College, 1766; died 1794.

Francis Hopkinson: born in Philadelphia, September 21, 1737; graduated Princeton College, 1763; admitted to the bar, 1765; collector of customs at New Castle, Del., 1772; resided at Bordentown, N. J.; member of Congress, 1776–1777; treasurer Continental loan office; judge of admiralty for Pennsylvania, 1779–1789; judge U. S. District Court, 1790–1791; died at Philadelphia, May 9, 1791.

John Hart: son of Edward; born in Hopewell Township, N. J., 1708; farmer; member of Provincial Legislature for several years; member of Congress, 1774–1776; chairman of the New Jersey Council of Safety, 1777–1778; first clerk of the New Jersey State Assembly; popularly known as "Honest John Hart"; died at Hopewell, May 11, 1779.

Abraham Clark: born 1726; famous as "poor man's lawyer"; sheriff of Newark; died, 1794, buried at Rahway, N. J.

TWO FAMOUS MEN OF BURLINGTON

Burlington, New Jersey, is the birthplace of two famous men.   Here at 459 South High Street, Captain James Lawrence was born, October 1, 1781.   And, in the house on the left, next door to him, James Fennimore Cooper was born, September 15, 1789.

When James Lawrence grew up he became an officer in the United States Navy.   He commanded the American frigate, *Chesapeake*, during the War of 1812.

In the battle between the *Chesapeake* and the British ship *Shannon*, he was mortally wounded. The following poem entitled "Grandfather's Rhyme" tells of his brave death:

When I was but a boy,
  I heard the people tell
How gallant Captain Lawrence
  So bravely fought and fell.

The ships lay close together,
  I heard the people say,
And many guns were roaring
  Upon that battle day.

A grape-shot struck the captain
  He laid him down to die:
They say the smoke of powder
  Made dark the sea and sky.

The sailors heard a whisper
  Upon the captain's lip:
The last command of Lawrence
  Was, "Don't give up the ship."

And ever since that battle
  The people like to tell
How gallant Captain Lawrence
  So bravely fought and fell.

When disappointment happens,
  And fear your heart annoys,
Be brave, like Captain Lawrence—
  And don't give up, my boys!

The *Chesapeake* was defeated but the brave words of Captain Lawrence were remembered by the Americans. In a later battle, during the same war, Captain Perry— later Commodore Perry—was in command of the *Lawrence* named for Captain Lawrence.   Before going into battle, he unfurled his battle flag: a blue square on which in white letters were the words "DON'T GIVE UP THE SHIP."   This was the motto with which Captain Perry began his famous victory of Lake Erie. That same flag, today, hangs in the Naval Academy at Annapolis; and that motto is the motto of all the midshipmen who are fortunate enough to go to Uncle

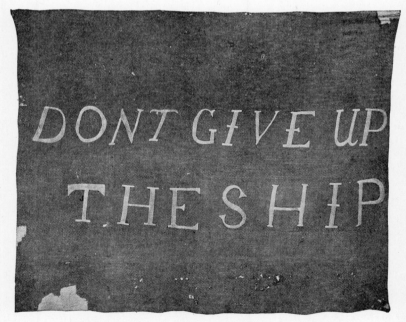

PERRY'S FLAG AT THE BATTLE OF LAKE ERIE

Sam's training school—the dying words of a brave Jerseyman: "Don't Give Up the Ship."

*   *   *   *   *   *

James Fenimore Cooper became famous as a writer. Perhaps one of his books is already a favorite of yours. He wrote the *Leatherstocking Tales*, a series of exciting adventure stories of frontiersmen and Indians. His story of the young chief, Uncas, *The Last of the Mohicans* is particularly good. If you have not already read this book, you have a real treat coming to you.

The birthplace of the author of these tales, James Fenimore Cooper, is, now, owned and occupied by the Burlington County Historical Society. This, but not the house next door, the birthplace of Captain James Lawrence, is open for public inspection.

BARNEGAT LIGHT

Barnegat Lighthouse, situated on the northern end of Twelve Mile Beach, is one of the primary lighthouses on the Atlantic Coast. It was built in 1858.

It is a red and white tower; 161 feet high; equipped with a lens, having a bull's-eye in the center, 18 inches in diameter. Were it not for the curve of the earth's surface, its powerful light, equal to 30,000,000 candle power, could be seen by sailors one hundred miles from shore.

A few years ago, the ocean had washed away so much land that the entire tower was in grave danger of toppling into the sea. Lovers of the old light collected money and old automobiles and scrap iron. The money was used to put in heavy iron pilings

Courtesy Esso Tours and W. W. Tupper

SUNSET, BARNEGAT BAY

BARNEGAT LIGHT

around the base of the lighthouse, and the old automobiles and scrap iron were thrown into the ocean to build a bulwark against the ocean waves. The old light was saved, though it still leans a little toward the sea.

Lighthouses are controlled by the Bureau of Lighthouses, Department of Commerce of the Federal Government. Barnegat Light is in the third lighthouse district.

It is, now, a State Museum.

CAPTAIN KIDD

The New Jersey coast with its many small islands, sand dunes, ground pine, and gravelly beaches is a fit setting for stories of pirates. And many stories of pirates there are.

The stories of Captain Kidd are perhaps the most plentiful. His ship the *Quedagh Merchant* is said to have stopped several times at various places. Shark River, between Belmar and Bradley Beach, is supposed to have been a stopping-place of his. It is fact that he did put in to Stites Beach, now Cape May Point, several times. One of his landings here is mentioned in a report of the Lords of Trade to the Lords Justices dated August 10, 1669. There was an old tree, known as Kidd's Tree, near the lighthouse there until

KIDD'S JOLLY ROGER

CAPTAIN KIDD'S
SIGNATURE

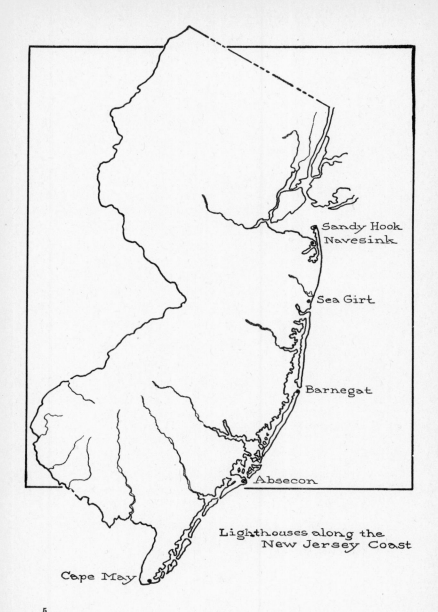

Sandy Hook
Navesink

Sea Girt

Barnegat

Absecon

Lighthouses along the
New Jersey Coast

Cape May

about 1893.   What gruesome or common-place story is behind that name!

Just what the purpose of the pirates was in making their landings is unknown.   Tales of buried treasure have given rise to treasure hunts which have taken place at various times all along the coast of New Jersey from Cooper's Ferry to Navesink.

The value of Kidd's treasure was between £40,000 and £50,000 or $200,000 and $250,000.   Of this, something over £10,000 or $50,000 has been recovered.

If you wish to go on a treasure hunt of your own, I can promise some good exercise, lots of fun, and who knows—perhaps—buried treasure!

SEE OYSTER FLEET AT BIVALVE

Bivalve Boats Special Sight in June
News Item

Place: Maurice River or Bivalve, New Jersey (C-12 on your 1933 Esso map).

Time: Any Sunday afternoon in June (preferably warm and sunny with light breezes).

Characters: Some three hundred oyster boats, plus an admiring audience of Esso motorists.

And what a picturesque sight it is to watch the trim, white boats of the entire oyster fleet drifting silently out of the harbor under full sail during mid-afternoon.

May and June are the two months when dredging is permitted on the State-owned beds.   Young "seed oysters" are gathered to be transplanted to private grounds and carefully nursed into juicy, tasty bivalves.   The boats are restricted to sail power to prevent excessive and destructive dredging.   For the other ten months of the year the sails are carefully stowed away, and the boats operate under power.   So be sure to visit Bivalve this month—and don't forget the camera if you'd like to get some pictures as lovely as anything an artist could paint.

—Esso Tours

Courtesy Esso Tours and W. W. Klenke

PICTURESQUE SCENES, SUCH AS THIS GREET THE TOURISTS
ALONG THE MAURICE RIVER AND DELAWARE BAY

Courtesy Ewing Galloway

OYSTER FLEET ON DELAWARE BAY AT BIVALVE

SOUTH JERSEY PRODUCES HOLLY

Holly trees are considered to be weather prophets. When they have few berries, old-timers say that the winter will be mild.   When the berries are plentiful, the winter will be a severe one.

It is difficult to believe that at one time holly trees were destroyed as nuisances by farmers until someone thought of shipping the cheerful evergreen to cities for Christmas decorations.

It was about 1890 that South Jersey farmers first began to realize that holly could be a paying crop. They began to sell the branches from their trees for Christmas decorations and wreaths instead of burning them.   In those days they got a dollar a case for it, but, today, they realize considerably more profit from their holly.

In medieval times, it is said, it was considered unlucky to gather holly out of season, because, before and after Christmas, it belonged to the wood elves. Today, motorists and hikers do well to remember that it is unlucky to gather it, even in season, because there are strict laws to protect it, and it may belong to a good marksman who owns dogs.

The clean white close-grained wood of the holly tree is much in demand for inlay work and wood patterns, and forms the "ebony" handle on many a teapot. For making a hot fire, farmers say that no wood can surpass holly. Birdlime, a sticky substance spread to snare or "lime" small birds, is still made from holly bark.

The ancients believed that holly possessed mystic power that enabled it to freeze water and subdue wild animals. Zoroastrians believed that the sun never cast a shadow from it; legend tells us that lightning will not strike us if we carry a bit of holly in our pocket. But, today, the bright-berried scratchy sprays signify to all the full good cheer of the Holiday Season from far Hollywood to our own Mount Holly.

WHEN BETSY ELOPED TO GLOUCESTER

Betsy Griscom was as pretty a little Quaker maid as ever lived in Philadelphia. She was not too short and not too tall, with brown hair and sparkling blue eyes. Her cheeks were pink with health. She was witty and attractive, popular and a leader among her friends.

Naturally a girl such as Betsy was, twenty years old, had masculine as well as feminine admirers. Three, did Betsy have: John Ross, Joseph Ashburn, and John Claypoole. All these young men were of good family and good character.

But Betsy's father looked with disfavor on them all because none of them were of Betsy's religion—that of the Friends or Quakers. When Betsy began to favor John Ross, the Griscoms became much annoyed, because John Ross's father was assistant rector of Christ Episcopal Church. The Episcopal Church or Church of England had helped a great deal in the persecution of the Quakers in England, so that in the eyes of her father, John Ross was the least desirable of the three.

It is said, "Forbidden fruit tastes the sweetest," and certain it is that Betsy and John became more and more in love with each other.

Many a moonlight night the lovers strolled along the shore of the Delaware. Whenever there were picnics to Chestnut Hill or Germantown or sailing parties to

Burlington or Bordentown, John and Betsy were together.

When Betsy went to market, which she did nearly every morning, she stopped at the upholsterer's shop, where her beloved John was apprenticed, to see how he was getting on with his work.

One day, Betsy announced to her family that she had promised to marry John Ross. Her father stormed, her mother wept. In vain, did they remind her that did she marry a man of a different religion from her own, she would be read out of meeting (that is, she would no longer be allowed to attend the Friend's Meeting or Church). She held firm in her love for John.

Finally the young people, despairing that they would be allowed to wed at home, decided to elope. Betsy has just passed twenty-one and both were now of age. John had a friend in Gloucestertown, now Gloucester, William Hugg, Jr., who promised to help the couple.

HUGG'S INN, GLOUCESTER, WHERE BETSY GRISCOM AND JOHN ROSS WERE MARRIED

To Gloucester, Betsy Griscom and John Ross went by ferry on the fourth of November, 1773, and there

BETSY ROSS HOUSE,
PHILADELPHIA, 1937

were married. William Hugg, Jr., the proprietor of Hugg's Inn, famous then for its hospitality and now famous in memory for the many famous people it housed, proved a real friend. In order to obtain a marriage license in New Jersey at that time, it was necessary for two people to go on a bond that the bride was twenty-one. One or both had to pledge £500 ($2,500) that this was true, and William Hugg, Jr., did that for his friend. The bond may be seen today signed by John Ross, William Hugg, Jr., and James Bowman, known as the marrying parson, in the records at the State House in Trenton, N. J.

The two lovers were married by the marrying parson, James Bowman, and it is fair to assume that the place was Hugg's Inn on the banks of the Delaware River, at Gloucester.

When she returned home, Betsy was read out of meeting as she had been promised. Thereafter she attended Christ Church in Philadelphia with John.

Betsy and John Ross opened a little upholstery shop to which General Washington came a few years later to ask Betsy Ross to make our first flag. Her husband had already given his life for his country. This house is known today as the Betsy Ross House, the birthplace of our flag.

THE MUD ROUNDS

The retreat through New Jersey, in November and December, 1776, has usually been called, by the veterans of that day, "The Mud Rounds." It was so called because of the condition of the roads which during the first part of the march, were almost impassable quagmires. Before the march was ended, this mud became frozen—an awful road, indeed, for barefooted soldiers, of whom there were many in the shrunken ranks of the Americans.

"I have talked with several soldiers," said Dr. Joseph F. Tuttle, in the 1840's, "who were in the Army during that retreat, and have read what Dr. Lewis Condict, who talked to more, had to say: all who were in that march alluded to the 'Mud Rounds' as a time of great suffering and hardship."

Old David Gordon, of Rockaway, who, at the age of ninety-two, was as cheerful as a bird, frequently spoke of that march with a shudder; and he was better off than many of his companions, for he had shoes for his feet.

There were other difficulties for the soldiers along that line of march. Their tents and clothing were insufficient to protect them. The roads were either muddy or frozen. The rainstorms were severe. And the inhabitants along the route, supposing the cause of Independence to be ruined, were panic-stricken.

And yet the weary, ragged regiments of Washington never distrusted him, who so well deserved their trust. He proved himself a true hero in this difficult time.

The "Mud Rounds" was the forerunner of the victories of Trenton, Assanpink, and Princeton. Washington said, "These victories have fired the Eastern Regiments with ardor to protract their time of service —and the Militia are pouring in from all quarters, and only want veteran troops to lead them on."

WASHINGTON'S CHRISTMAS GIFT TO HIS COUNTRY

When Washington was driven out of New York, in December, 1776, he and his brave soldiers were forced to flee across New Jersey to the Delaware River which they crossed just above Trenton. They crossed to the Pennsylvania side in order to place the barrier of the mighty river between themselves and the Hessians at Trenton.

The Americans were without warm houses. Their only shelter was whatever they could build for themselves out of logs, stones, or earth. Their clothes were ragged and worn. For shoes, many had rags wound around their legs and feet. To make matters worse, they had little food and that irregularly. It was not everyone who would help a nearly defeated army. Their food was supplied by the forage troops—their hunting grounds, the country around the camp.

McKONKEY FERRY HOUSE, WASHINGTON'S CROSSING PARK

In this house many a colonial soldier was warmed and sheltered on that cold and snowy Christmas night. It is located on the New Jersey side of the Delaware River.

When the river froze over, the protection which it offered the discouraged patriots would be gone. The Hessians well realizing this, waited on the other side of the river, licking their chops like so many cats at a mouse-hole. Everyone knew that when the Hessians fought the Americans, the patriot army would be broken, Washington would be defeated, America's hope of liberty would be lost.

The Hessians knew this but—so did Washington. He had no wish to sit still and be crushed. He knew, also, the Hessian soldiers. He knew what great store the German places on his Christmas feast, with what abundance he loads his table with rich foods and wines, and how he loves to stuff himself on this great holiday.

General Washington had figured out a plan of escape, a desperate one it is true. His spies had brought him information that made him believe that

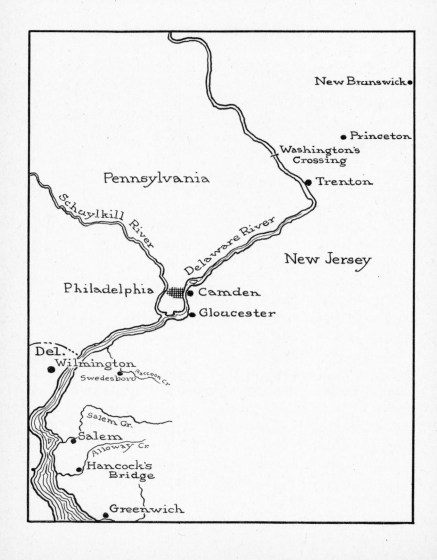

he might succeed.   He decided that Christmas Night was the time to carry it out.

The Hessians were singing, eating, and drinking Christmas Day and far into Christmas Night, until, indeed, many of them had fallen into stuffed and drunken sleep.

While this was going on, the Americans marched up the river bank, got onto flatboats at McKonkey's Ferry and, taking their few cannon with them, poled the boats across the river at what is now known as *Washington's Crossing*.   There were great pieces of ice in the bitter cold water.   The men were poorly dressed. Some had no shoes.   The icy frozen ground cut them, the frost bit them and the bloody footmarks on the ground bore mute testimony to their sufferings.

It was three o'clock in the morning after Christmas, when the last boatload crossed the river.   It was hailing and snowing and bitter cold.   Two of the soldiers were frozen to death.

Courageously pushing on, encouraged by their brave leader, and the hope of escape from their trap, they reached Trenton about eight o'clock in the morning.

As the tired men sighted the small wooden houses with the wisps of smoke curling upwards from the chimneys, Washington faced about in his saddle, waved his sword and said: "Yonder, my brave fellows, are the enemies of your country!   Remember what you are fighting for!"

The Hessians were surprised and utterly confused. They were defeated though they fought bravely.

The battle lasted about two hours, though the actual fighting was less than an hour.

The victory cheered the people in all the colonies and was a real gift of cheer and hope to the struggling young nation from its great General George Washington.

THE OLD BARRACKS AT TRENTON

The Old Barracks are located at the corner of South Willow Street and Front Street, near by the State Capitol Building and the Delaware River.

The original sections of the building were erected in 1758 by petition of the people to house the King's troops in order to protect the people from the Indians, during the French and Indian War.

For two weeks before the battle of Trenton, English dragoons and German yagers, along with some Tory refugees, occupied the building.

TRENTON BARRACKS
Original section built, 1758, to house troops of French and Indian War.

A week after the battle of Trenton, the building was filled with American militia.

Today it is used largely as a museum and contains many relics of Colonial times. It is under the management of the Old Barracks Association; several patriotic societies such as the Daughters of Colonial Wars of New Jersey, the Daughters of the American Revolution, and Sons of the Revolution meet in this historical spot.

There was an exact replica of the Old Barracks built at the Sesqui-Centennial Exposition in Philadelphia in 1926 and was named the New Jersey House.

OLD NASSAU

At Princeton, New Jersey, is located the fourth oldest chartered college, now university, in the United States; Harvard, William and Mary College, and Yale, being the first three. The charter of Princeton College was granted in 1746.

Its oldest building, Nassau Hall, cost £2900, or about $14,500. It was four stories high and one hundred seventy-five feet long—the largest stone building in the colonies when it was built in 1756.

Nassau Hall has served many purposes besides that of education for which it was built. Its original paved halls have resounded to the laughter of students engaged in mischievous pranks: dragging a calf up the stairs and turning it loose; or rolling heated cannon balls down the length of the corridors.

When the Revolutionary War began it affected the classes at the college. The Commencement Exercises

OLD NASSAU, PRINCETON

in June, 1776, were held at Cooper's Ferry, now Camden. This was the only meeting of the Trustees of Princeton College held out of Princeton because of the war. Many of the students joined Washington's army; and finally, the few who remained at school were sent away early in January, 1777, just in time to avoid the British, who took possession of Nassau Hall on the third of January.

Still later, General Israel Putnam, of the American Army, used the building as a barracks, a hospital, and a military prison.

The Continental Congress met in Nassau Hall for five months in 1783. Here, George Washington was summoned to receive the official thanks of the colonies for his brave deeds. "In other nations, many have performed eminent services, for which they have deserved the thanks of the public. But to you, Sir, peculiar praise is due. Your services have been essential in acquiring and establishing the freedom and independence of your country. They deserve the grateful acknowledgments of a free and independent nation."

It was at this same commencement that General Washington made a gift to Princeton College of £50 ($250).

This money was later used to buy a portrait of the giver by Charles Willson Peale. Peale painted many pictures of Washington but this particular one is a full-length portrait. In the background is depicted the battle of Princeton, with General Mercer lying wounded and bleeding. This portrait was placed in the frame from which a British cannon ball shot the picture of George II, during the battle of Princeton, in 1777.

Today, Princeton men sing "In praise of old Nassau, my boys, Hurrah! Hurrah! Hurrah! Her sons shall give, while they shall live, Three cheers for old Nassau."

RED BANK

Near the partially identified site of Fort Nassau along the Delaware River, below Gloucester, Fort Mercer was built in 1777. It was named for General Hugh Mercer who died in the battle of Princeton, January 3 of that year. This was part of a series of defenses of Philadelphia that were built to protect that city from the reported advances of the British.

On August 1, 1777, General Washington inspected Fort Mifflin (Mud Island), Fort Mercer (Red Bank), Billingsport, and Marcus Hook.

August 23, Washington returned to Philadelphia. The American Army and the British Army met in the Battle of Brandywine on September 11. On September 21, General Howe continued his victorious march to Philadelphia. That city was formally occupied by the British on September 26. The Americans took up their winter quarters, not far away, at Valley Forge.

To secure control of the Delaware River to the British, Lord Richard Howe, brother to Sir William Howe, sailed up the river with his fleet. At Billingsport, he was stopped by a naval stockade built of poles, thirty to forty feet long, driven into the mud. At the top of each pole was fastened a long, sharp piece of iron for the purpose of piercing the bottom of any vessel that might try to sail over the obstruction. This stockade extended from Billingsport to Red Bank.

Captain Hammond of the British ship, *Roebuck*, volunteered to break a way through this defence if a sufficient force of men were sent to Billingsport and Red Bank to capture those points.

At Billingsport, the Americans believing themselves overwhelmed, spiked their guns, set fire to the barracks, and fled. The British, then, broke a seven-foot passage through the stockade, sailed six of their smaller vessels through and anchored in the Delaware just below Red Bank.

Upon Fort Mifflin, Fort Mercer, and the small ships of the Americans, fell the responsibility of checking the advance of the British fleet and the protection of western New Jersey.

At Fort Mercer were two Rhode Island regiments of four hundred men, commanded by Colonel Christopher Greene. Colonel Greene had not enough men to defend the entire fort; he blocked off part of it and proceded to strengthen the defenses as best he could with branches, hay, old lumber, board fences, and wooden pickets.

Scarcely had Colonel Greene completed his fortifications when two thousand Hessian troops under Count Carl Emil Kurt von Donop were sent from Philadelphia to capture Fort Mercer. Part of their route to Red Bank is still known as Hessian Road.

On the twenty-second of October, the Hessians arrived at Fort Mercer and after demanding under flag of truce that the rebel forces lay down their arms, and receiving an abrupt refusal, attacked the fort. The British ships aided in the cannonading. The *Augusta*, the *Roebuck*, and the *Merlin* endeavored to attract the attention of the American ships in order to keep them from assisting the fort.

The Hessians advanced to the first trench; finding it abandoned, they rushed in. It was a trap—terrific volleys of cannon and rifle fire mowed them down. Their brave commander, Count von Donop (and a courageous enemy is always to be honored), rallied his men. But they were driven back after terrific loss. A gallant Frenchman, Monsieur du Plessis Mauduit, sallying forth from the fort to repair some fortifications, heard a voice from among heaps of dead and dying asking, "Draw me hence." He did, and found that the badly wounded man was Count von Donop. He was carefully carried to the fort, but later removed to a near-by house, where he died three days later. The leaderless Hessians fled.

The following day the attack upon the fort by the British ships was renewed. The *Augusta* ran aground, and was set on fire. The *Merlin* met the same fate. The *Roebuck* survived the battle but several years later was wrecked on Absecon Beach, N. J. For many years the gaunt ribs of the British ship *Augusta* could be seen just off shore near the site of Fort Mercer.

By Act of Congress, twenty acres of land including the site of Fort Mercer, monuments, and the site of the Whitall house were converted into a public park under the care of the Gloucester County Board of Freeholders.

At National Park, as it is known today, you may visit Red Bank Battlefield, and construct again, for yourself, the actions of our brave patriots and our courageous enemies.

ANN WHITALL

The house of Isaac and Ann Whitall stands just south of Red Bank Battlefield. It was built twenty-nine years before the construction of Fort Mercer.

On the day of the battle, the rest of the Whitall family took refuge in a safe place, but the stanch Quakeress, Ann, would not go. When entreated by her grandson to come with them, she said, "The Lord will take just as good care of me here as anywhere else." She continued her spinning during the rain of shot and shell, until one cannon ball pierced the wall, narrowly missed her and lodged in a partition near by. This proved too much for her. Deciding to mix prudence with faith, she picked up her spinning wheel and retreated to the cellar, where she went on with her work till the end of the battle, which lasted about three quarters of an hour.

Her house was used as a hospital, and Ann herself helped nurse the wounded, it is said, soundly scolding the Hessian wounded for coming to America to fight the Americans.

ANN WHITALL HOUSE
The house faces the Delaware.

NEW JERSEY'S PRESIDENTS

While New Jersey cannot lay claim to being the Home of Presidents, as Virginia does, still she can claim for her own, two sons who became Presidents of the United States: Stephen Grover Cleveland, a native son; and Thomas Woodrow Wilson, an adopted son. Both served two terms as president, both were lawyers by profession, both are better known by their middle and last names.

Grover Cleveland was born in Caldwell, Essex County, New Jersey, on March 18, 1837. He was the son of a Presbyterian minister and the fifth child in a family of nine children.

When Grover Cleveland was very young his family removed to New York State, where he spent most of his life. He was elected Governor of New York State in 1882 by a large majority. He was so successful in this office that he was elected president, two years later. He was a man who believed that to break faith was unforgiveable. He proved a trustworthy officer. He was succeeded in the presidency by Benjamin Harrison, but was elected for his second term in 1892. On March 4, 1897, he retired to Princeton, New Jersey, where he lived until his death, June 24, 1908.

It is interesting to note that Woodrow Wilson wrote several articles on "Cleveland as President" while he himself was still a private citizen. Woodrow Wilson was born in Staunton, Virginia, on December 28, 1856. He graduated from Princeton University in 1879. In 1890, he returned to Princeton University as a member of the faculty, teaching Law. In 1902, he became President of the University and continued to hold this office until he retired from school work in 1910. He was elected governor of New Jersey in 1910; and in 1912, he was elected President of the United States. He held this office for two terms, until March 4, 1921.

His term of office was an eventful one. The World War took place during that time. Due to his activities during the war and following that at the Peace Conference which he attended in person, his health broke, leaving him a partly paralyzed invalid. He spent the remainder of his life in Washington, D. C., where he died three years after his retirement. He is buried in the Westminster Abbey of America—the National Cathedral of Saint Peter and Saint Paul at Mount St. Albans, Washington.

PETER KALM DESCRIBES NEW BRUNSWICK IN 1748

We continued our journey from Trenton to New Brunswick, in the morning, the country through which we passed was for the greatest part level, though sometimes there were some long hills, some parts covered

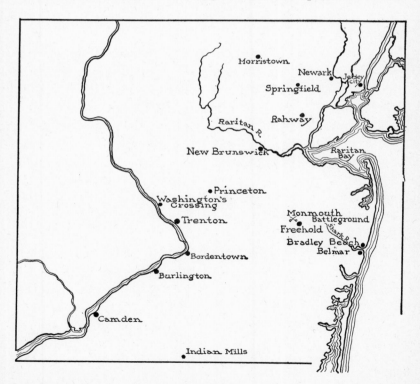

with trees, but far the greater part of the country was without woods; on the other hand, I never saw any place in America, the towns excepted, so well peopled. An old man, who lived in this neighborhood and accompanied us for some part of the road, however, assured me, that he could well remember the time, when between Trenton and New Brunswick, there were not more than three farms.

During the greater part of the day we had very extensive corn fields on both sides of the road. Near almost every farm was a spacious orchard full of peach and apple trees, and in some of them the fruit had fallen from the trees in such quantities, as to cover nearly the whole surface. Part of it, they left to rot, since they could not use all of it.

Wherever we passed by we were always welcome to go into the fine orchards, and gather our hats and pockets full of the choicest fruit, without the possessors so much as looking after it.

THE JERSEY BLUES

In the first year of the war, uniforms were almost unknown in the American Army. Sometimes even the necessities of clothing, such as shoes, were lacking. The soldiers were obliged, for the most part, to furnish their own weapons.

Sometimes patriotic citizens would send what clothing they could to the army. Often, they banded together to prepare clothing to give to the soldiers.

One such group was composed of women in the township of Springfield, New Jersey, who furnished a regiment from their neighborhood with tow frocks and breeches dyed a bright blue. From the color of their uniforms they were named "The Jersey Blues."

Later during the war, the army was better supplied with both arms and uniforms. As the young republic grew older, it was enabled to purchase the things needful to it.

HANS VAN PELT

Hans Van Pelt was an honest low-Dutchman;
Not low in his stature, but low by the Van
That you find in his name and which proves his descent
From the burghers of old, who, with peaceful intent,
From the Indians bought all the valleys along
The Raritan, and the Musconetcong;
A long belt of land that runs from the West,
From where Delaware joins with the laughing Pequest,
To the East where Passaic, or Hackensack flows,
And Communipaw rests in its quiet repose.

In the days of our fathers, New Brunswick was known
Through all this broad belt as the chief market town,
And thither our farmers oft wended their way
With their barley and oats, and their long wains of hay;
And such stories they told by their bright Winter fires
That each lad in the land longed to see its tall spires.

So one day, as noon's shadows to rosy tints melt,
That bold son of Neshanic, young, burly, Van Pelt,
On horse ventured forth for this city so gay.
Joy gleamed from his eyes as he rode on his way;

But a sad thought at times drove its light from his
    face—
The thought that Lord Howe might soon capture the
    place;
For of all things under the sun or the moon,
The most fearful to him was a British Dragoon.

When many a farm house and hamlet were passed;
When the shadows of day had so shortened their cast,
That the reaching foreleg of the horse in its tread
Stood over the shade of the animal's head,
From the brow of a high hill he saw at his feet
New Brunswick, above which the hazy smoke curled
From many a forge; while beyond, with sails furled,
Rode long schooners and brigs, from the marts of the
    world.

There afar flowed the Raritan winding its way
Through long meadows and marshes to Amboy Bay;
And there down in the waters reflected were seen
The wild blossoms in bloom on its borders of green,
For so lovely the wild flowers were blushing in bliss
Where daily the ocean runs up for a kiss;
Where, with shoulder to shoulder, the river and sea
Push their way through the reeds, and across the
    green lea,
Till the wavelets, all standing tip-toe on the shores,
With their cool lips just touch the warm lips of the
    flowers;
Where the river and sea, in a bright silver tide,
From the blossoms that deck the smooth meadowlands
    glide,

GREAT STATE HIGHWAY ALONG THE MUSCONETCONG

And soft sighs, and low sobs all the little waves heave,
While each tardily moves, as if loathing to leave,
Till, increasing in speed, they, in quick-pulsing swells,
Go far down to the bay, passing hills and fair dells.
For a romp on the beach with the wild sea's gay
    shells.

With knees pressing the saddle, erect in his seat
Hans rode into town through long Albany Street
Where he gazed with fresh joy at the tall stately stores
All with large, painted signs overhanging their doors,
So distinctly each lettered on wood, or on tin;
Without asking he knew who were merchants within.

In the heart of the city appeared to his ken
The endless long line of fair women and men,
And though bells were not ringing he had not a doubt
That service, was over, and church was just out,
And surmised, as he gazed on the gaily dressed crowd,
That New Brunswick's fine town-folks were all over-
    proud
In not giving to strangers that shake of the hand
That plain folks would give in Neshanic's green land.

At a window where brokers pile high their bright gold
He was gazing, and dreaming of riches untold,
When he heard a voice cry, "The British have come!"
Then approaching him near the clear tap of the drum.
Soon quivered the air to the bugle's loud blast,
And in martial array came a squad marching fast—
Not the soldiers of Howe and in red coats of flame,
But wild urchins, who mimicked war's blustering game.

On perceiving them Hans was so stricken with fear
That each boy in the ranks seemed a tall grenadier;
Each gay feather a plume and each broomstick a gun,
With a bayonet flashing the light of the sun.

Then the whip and the spur with wild vigor applying,
Up long Albany Street he rode galloping, flying
Far away from the foeman who had taken the town.
With a hand on the pommel to hold his weight down,
He rode galloping, flying past meadow and wood,
With the wild fear of danger ever chilling his blood,
And as thus he rode on, like as aspen he shook
When he turned in his saddle behind him to look,
For a cloud of red dust that arose in his rear
Seemed a British dragoon at a charge with a spear.

As in his mad flight he was riding adown
The broad highway that leads to old Middlebush town,
Some stray cows that were grazing along the roadside
The wild horse and his rider in wonderment eyed;
And when started the leader, alarmed at the sight,
With long tails high in air, the whole herd took to flight,
And then swiftly together pell-mell they came down
Horse, rider, and cows on old Middlebush town;
While the citizens hearing the noise and the clatter
From their houses all ran to see what was the matter;
And perceiving the cloud wreath they knew that there
    must
Be strong wind in its folds to uphold the red dust.

'Twas a whirling tornado, destruction in wrath,
Such as sweeps the green fields, as it speeds on its path,
Bare as lands in the east that the locusts encamp on,
On the fields through which ran the red foxes of Sampson.

But before a man moved, a fresh breeze in the air
Uncovered the legs that were galloping there,
When the gleaming sharp point of each curving cow
    horn
Seemed the point of a lance by an enemy borne.

Then arose a wild cry that rang far through the town,
That the Tories in hot wrath were fast riding down.
Such a racket, and tumult, and terrible roar
Never Middlebush heard neither since or before.

When his tired horse at last to the spur gave no heed,
And in vain strove the rider to quicken his speed,
As the day hid its face under night's sable gown,
On a slow-walk he rode into Millstone's fair town,
Where Ten Eycks, and Ten Broecks, and ten dozen
    or more
Of Van Dams and Van Liews, of Van Duzens, Van
    Dor-
Ens, Van Veghtens, Van Camps, Van Arsdales, Van
    Dycks,
Van Cleefs, and Van Syckles, Van Hornes and Van
    Slykes,
Who, that evening as wont having finished their chores,
Were all gathered in groups, just in front of their
    doors;
The men smoking and joking; the good women
    knitting—
An employment they follow, whether standing or
    sitting.
Salutations they gave Hans, believing the stranger
One riding the land with war's tiding of danger.

COVERED BRIDGE OVER THE NESHANIC AT MONTGOMERY

This bridge was recently replaced by a modern steel structure

Came his words to their ears, like chill winds to the
    flowers,
When an iceberg has stranded on tropical shores—
"The British have come!"—then, on turning his head
And beholding the moon, which now arid and red,
Hung low in the east, and shone through the dim haze—
"New Brunswick is sacked! See, the town's in a blaze,
And on their swift horses they hitherward come,
The soldiers of Howe to pillage your town."

Then the hardy Ten Broecks were all in a quiver,
Through the bold Ten Eycks swept an aching cold
    shiver,
And the tremor contagious spread to each man
Till aching and shaking stood every Van.

Trusty scouts were sent forward who rode all the night
Nor returned to the town till the dawn's early light,
Though far they had ridden, some to Brunswick below,
They found in the land not a sign of the foe.
Then the Vans took to swearing and swore all the day,
If ever again Hans should ride down that way,
Though he came like a priest, in a cassock and gown,
Only his ghost should ride forth from the town.

At midnight Hans reached the high hill of Neshanic,
Where he sprang from his horse and ran in his panic
To a cave on its brow, where long hidden he lay.
What came of him then, I really can't say,
For like the old dame, who lived under the hill,
For all that I know he is living there still.

                     —JOSEPH HUNT MILLER

OLD TENNENT

Photo by Chichester

OLD TENNENT CHURCH

The original church was built in 1731, but was replaced by the present building in 1750.

Near the church the famous Battle of Monmouth was fought on Sunday, June 28, 1778, between the Americans led by Washington and Lee, and the British led by General Henry Clinton. On that Sabbath day the usual preaching service was not held because of the lack of a pastor. A battle was expected in the neighborhood and women and children had been taken into hiding.

About noon of that day, General Washington came hurrying along the road about a hundred yards from the church door, with some six thousand men to join

7

Photo by Chichester

TWO GRAVE MARKERS IN OLD TENNENT CHURCHYARD

the battle.   He arrived on the field in time to turn
about the retreating Americans.   The main fighting
occurred about half way between Freehold and Old
Tennent Church.   The public highway and the Pennsylvania Railroad now pass over the battlefield.

The English records of the Battle of Monmouth say
that: "When Sir Henry (Clinton) was induced by
Lee to turn and fight on June 28, the heat of the weather
in that season always intense, was on that particular
day so great as to be seldom equaled even in the hot
summers of that continent, so that the troops were
already before the battle greatly fatigued.   The
position of the army, however, was critical and made
strong action necessary.   Sir Henry Clinton brought

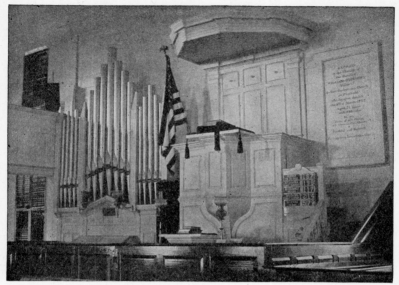

Photo by Chichester

OLD TENNENT CHURCH, INTERIOR

part of his second line and made some other plans to attack the enemy, but the army, in general, was now so overpowered by heat and fatigue that upon consideration he thought it better not to press the affair further.   He was, also, by this time confident that the purpose which had induced him to turn and attack was gained in saving his troops.   The battle was rendered grievous by the death of Colonel Monckton. That gallant officer, who had often met death in all its forms had the fortune of although being more than once severely wounded, both in other wars and the present, and after the hairbreadth escapes recovering when left among the dead on the field, was only reserved to be killed on this day, at the head of the second battalion of Grenadiers. This day and battle were also made famous by the singular circumstance, unequaled even in the history of the New World, of fifty-nine soldiers perishing without receiving a wound merely through the excessive heat and fatigue. Several of the Americans, also, accustomed as they were to the climate, died through the same cause."

Over the body of Lieutenant-Colonel Monckton, who was killed near the old parsonage of the church, was a desperate struggle until finally the Americans secured possession of it, carried it to the rear, brought it to the churchyard, and buried it a few feet from the southwest corner of the present church. Today, beside the body of Lieutenant-Colonel Monckton rests that of an American soldier who died in the same battle. Each Decoration Day, a British flag is placed on the grave of the British soldier and an American flag is placed on that of the American soldier.

During the battle the church was pierced by balls, the marks of which were allowed to remain for patriotic reasons, until it became necessary to repair the damage in order to preserve the building. As late as December, 1916, four cannon balls were dug up in the church ground during some grading operations. Stains of blood from a dying American soldier may still be seen on one of the pews of the church, to which, we are told, he was taken after being wounded by a spent ball. The church building was used, also, as a hospital after the battle by the Americans.

Today, when you visit this church, you may see the cannon balls which have been dug up, the blood-stained pew, and may read with interest the name plates on which are inscribed the names of those who have earned the honor in the service of their country.

MOLLY PITCHER IN THE BATTLE OF MONMOUTH

MOLLY PITCHER

During the Battle of Monmouth, John Hays, a gunner in the American Army, was shot down. His wife, Mary Ludwig Hays, a Pennsylvania German woman, who had been bringing water to the thirsty soldiers picked up the sponge-staff that he dropped as he fell, and aided in loading and firing that cannon until the end of the battle.

Washington made Mrs. Hays, better known as Molly Pitcher, a sergeant in the Continental Army in recognition of her services to her country.

There is a well on Monmouth Battlefield from which she is supposed to have brought water. Some people

MONUMENT ERECTED IN MEMORY OF MOLLY PITCHER, AT CARLISLE, PA.

say that Molly Pitcher's well was not really a well but a spring a short distance from the marker which is situated near where the Pennsylvania Railroad passes today.

After the battle, Molly Pitcher, took her wounded husband back to Carlisle, Pennsylvania, where he died.   She married, later, Sergeant George McCauley.

When she died on January 22, 1832, she was buried with military honors.

A beautiful monument was erected at Carlisle in her memory by the State of Pennsylvania on June 28, 1916, one hundred thirty-eight years after her brave deed.

CAPTAIN HUDDY

Electric refrigerators, tin cans, and such means of preserving food, so that it might be fit to eat, were entirely unknown at the time of the American Revolution. Salt took the place of these very modern preservatives. As there were no salt mines in the thirteen colonies, salt had to be made from water taken from the Atlantic Ocean.

During the war, soldiers must be fed well-preserved food which would not make them sick. Food was preserved by "curing" it with salt, or by smoking it.

It was necessary that new salt supplies should be procured by establishing salt works at various places. One of these was at Toms River. Thomas Savadge was the first manager of this factory. To protect this valuable industry and the small village of Toms River, a blockhouse was built and a small garrison of soldiers established there.

During the war the salt from Toms River Salt Works helped to keep the soldiers well and fit to fight for the cause of Liberty.

Cornwallis was defeated at Yorktown, October 19, 1781. The war was drawing to a close. At that time there were no telephones, telegraphs, radios, trains, airplanes, or steamships to rush news from one place to another. Many days were needed for news of importance to travel from one section of the country to another.

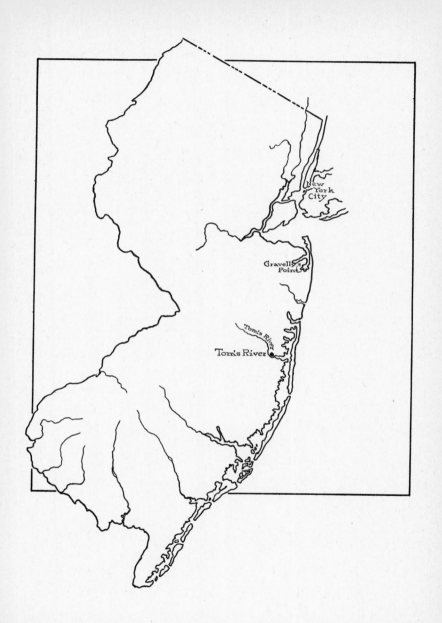

Captain Joshua Huddy, a brave and wise soldier, was in command of a little company of twenty-three men stationed at the blockhouse at Toms River.

Now, not all the people who had lived in the American colonies before the Revolution believed that the colonists should break away from the rule of the mother country, and some of the bitterest fighting was between men and women who had once lived as neighbors. Those who believed that the colonies should remain British were known as *Tories*. Some of these Tories, who had fled from their homes in New Jersey and the other colonies, formed bands of irregular soldiers who were known as *refugees*. While these refugees were not British soldiers, they did all that they could to defeat the American patriots. The Tories raided the Americans and the Americans raided the Tories. The Tories, however, were frequently more cruel and more heartless than seemed necessary even in raids on the patriotic colonists.

In the middle of March, 1782, nearly seven months after the battle of Yorktown, a band of forty refugees and a crew of eighty armed seamen set sail from New York City in whaleboats, accompanied by the brig *Arrogant*. Though delayed by high winds, they landed near Toms River about midnight of the twenty-third of March.

Here, they were joined by other refugees who were commanded by Richard Davenport and led by William Dillon, another refugee. By a northern route they headed for the fort. By taking this route, they escaped Captain Huddy's scouts, and completely surprised the Americans.

The Tories demanded that the Americans immediately surrender, and although Captain Huddy and his brave band were outnumbered four to one, they refused.

The fight which followed was brief but bloody. The fort was red with the blood of brave men, and two officers were dead. Thinking to save the lives of the rest and seeing inevitable defeat ahead, Captain Huddy surrendered.

The Tories burned the blockhouse and the village. The captives were placed aboard a boat and taken back to New York where they arrived the next day. Captain Huddy was placed in an old sugar house that was used as a prison.

Six days after Huddy was taken, a refugee Tory carpenter, named Philip White of Shrewsbury, was shot "while attempting to escape" from some Americans who had captured him. It is believed, however, that he was shot by one of the Americans whose father

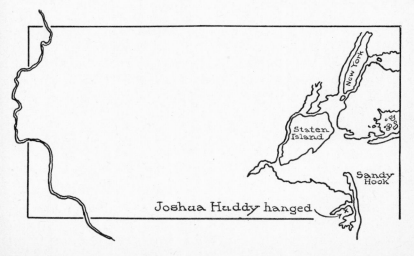

had been murdered by White and some other refugees some time before.

To retaliate, Captain Huddy was dragged from prison, hurried to Gravelly Point on the Navesink, near the old Highland Lighthouse. Here, on the shore of old Shrewsbury, a rude gallows was made of three rails and a barrel head. On this barrel head, Joshua Huddy hurriedly wrote his last will.

Now, Joshua Huddy was a good man and a brave soldier, and in no way was responsible for the death of Philip White. He deserved better than the death of a felon. Even the soldiers in this band did not have the brutalness to murder such a man, and refused to pull the rope that would take his life. But their commander, Richard Lippincott, with many harsh words, himself seized the rope and dragged aloft the body of the heroic patriot, Captain Huddy, whose last

THREE RAILS AND A BARREL HEAD

words were, "I shall die innocent and in a good cause."

Lippincott returned to New York and reported that on April 12, 1782, he had "exchanged" Captain Huddy for Philip White.

A brave soldier had given his life for the cause of liberty and freedom, after victory had been won— Captain Joshua Huddy, a soldier and a man!

RINGOES

Although nearly two million acres or nearly forty-five per cent of New Jersey is forested, a town which began where two paths through the woods crossed still has something of interest about it from that fact alone.

Thus did Ringoes begin, when John Ringo built his tavern at the crossing of woods paths in 1720. If it were possible to know the names of the travelers who stopped there for rest and refreshment, what a story it would make! Indians, traders, farmers, soldiers, and perhaps some of the European travelers who came to see how the Americans lived in the wilderness.

Ringoes was already growing old when the colonies rebelled and the American Revolution began.

In 1778 while the British were at Trenton, a party was sent out to destroy Flemington. When the British soldiers got as far as Pennington, a scouting party was sent out which was attacked when it reached Ringoes. Commander Geary, the British leader was killed and the rest of the party fled to New Brunswick, upon which the British retreated. Thanks to the patriots at Ringoes, Flemington was not destroyed.

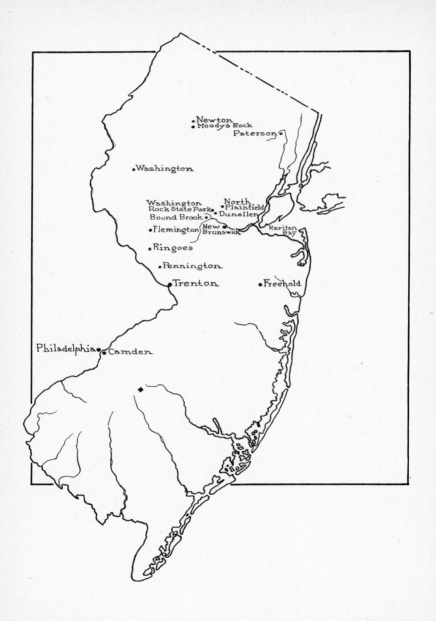

Newton
Moody's Rock
Paterson

Washington

Washington
Rock State Park
Bound Brook
Flemington
Ringoes
Pennington
Trenton

North
Plainfield
Dunellen
New
Brunswick
Raritan
Bay

Freehold

Philadelphia Camden

WASHINGTON ROCK

Along the Watchung Mountains, just northeast of Dunellen in Middlesex County, looking up the road between Bound Brook and North Plainfield, one may see the Stars and Stripes floating on the breeze. Following the road leading from Route 29 toward the flag, a mountain road leads one to Washington Rock.

A monument built of field stones stands there now, and tells the traveler that it was from this place that Washington watched the movements of the British fleet in Raritan Bay nearly twenty miles away. From here, too, he could see the movements of the contending armies in the plains below.

Aside from the fact that the great Washington stood on that rock and saw the same scenes (with the exception of the buildings that are now much more plentifully scattered over the landscape) that you may see if you go there, the view itself is well worth the climb to the top.

Just back of the "lookout," is a pleasant picnic grove. The entire spot, now, has been set aside by New Jersey as Washington Rock State Park.

MIDDLEBROOK

Washington first camped at Middlebrook upon leaving winter quarters in Morristown in 1777. He stayed at the Heights from late in May until late in June of that year.

The army was encamped upon the right of the road leading through the mountain gorge in which Chimney Rock is situated. A strong earthwork was thrown up about a quarter of a mile to the northwest, almost in the center of Washington Valley, as a protection against the possible approach of the British from the direction of Pluckemin; the whole of the defile leading through the narrow mountain valley was strongly guarded, while the brow overlooking the plain bristled with cannon. Just at the edge of the wood, east of Chimney Rock, huts were erected as quarters for the officers, and everything done which either safety or comfort demanded in the emergency. At Bound Brook a strong redoubt was constructed, commanding the bridge over that miry little stream, just north of the present railroad crossing, in case an attack was made from the direction of New Brunswick where the main force of the British lay. Having taken, in this way, all possible precautions against surprise, Washington felt safe to wait for whatever might happen. On the summit of the Round Top, on the left of the gorge in which Chimney Rock stands, there are yet to be seen rude remains of a hut which Washington sometimes frequented during those anxious months of 1777. The high points at Middlebrook formed valuable natural watchtowers for the Americans.

While the army was encamped here, Congress was in session at Philadelphia, not many miles away. The flag, which Mrs. Betsy Ross had fashioned for the new republic, had been presented to and adopted by that same Congress on the fourteenth of June, 1777. The anniversary of that day we now celebrate as Flag Day.

A courier was sent to Camp Middlebrook to inform the commander in chief that the cause for which he was fighting had adopted a National Flag and what that flag was. Accordingly, the army was summoned to the parade ground, and the Stars and Stripes were first displayed to the gaze of this group of men who were offering their lives and fortunes to make it the symbol of the great nation which, today, it stands for. Many years later the Legislature of the State of New Jersey provided money for a monument to mark this spot as the place where the Stars and Stripes were first presented to the army of the future United States of America.

Late in June the camp was broken and the army departed in pursuit of the British who had left New Brunswick, where they had spent some months, to embark at Sandy Hook for Philadelphia.

Remembering the lay of the land at Middlebrook, while arranging the encampment of his army for the winter of 1778–1779, Washington sent seven brigades there. On November 30, 1778, over eight thousand men came to the Heights of Middlebrook. General Washington arrived on December 11, 1778.

The General was offered the use of the Wallace House, which had been built that year and, indeed, was not yet entirely finished. He accepted. Mrs. Washington joined him there and spent the entire winter at Middlebrook. This house is preserved today as a museum and some of the rooms are kept just as they were when the Washingtons lived there. It is situated in Somerville near where the road to Raritan crosses the Central Railroad.

8

Other houses, also, had their illustrious occupants: General Nathanael Greene and his wife stayed at the Derick Van Veghten house on the Raritan—near the present station of Finderne; General von Steuben was at the Staats house on the south side of the Raritan near South Bound Brook.

The camp itself was in three parts.   General Washington says that one division "is on this side of Van Veghten's bridge on high grounds" (known as Mount Pleasant—northwest of the present Finderne station) the other two parts are upon the mountains over Bound Brook.

Washington wrote to Lafayette on March 8, 1779: "Our troops are in a more agreeable and fertile country than they were in last winter; and they are better clad and more healthy than they have ever been since the formation of the army."

The lowly huts of Middlebrook,
    Which sheltered from the storm
Those who from God their lesson took,
    Nor bowed to human form—
What glory gathers round the spot,
    Like aureola gleam!
And passing time eclipses not
    Of light that radiant stream.

The crowded huts of Middlebrook!
    Our Roman sires were there,
Who on the future dared to look,
    And knew not to despair.

'Mid autumn's foliage sere and dead,
  'Mid winter's snow and blast,
Hope, like the Eastern palm tree, spread,
  And flourished to the last.

Sequestered huts of Middlebrook!
  The nation's heart beat high,
When Clinton fled to Sandy Hook,
  And "Monmouth" was our cry.
And they who played the hero then
  Have passed to dust away,
And the log-built homes of truest men
  Have yielded to decay.

But hopes that rose at Middlebrook,
  And stern resolves, that there
Once murmured in a lowly nook,
  Are passing everywhere;
They speed around the earth, and shake
  The crumbling thrones of kings;
And despots start to cringe and quake,
  And feel like guilty things.

Oh! sainted hearts at Middlebrook,
  Your mission was sublime;
The cause you never once forsook
  Is bounded by no clime.
That cause—the cause of truth and right—
  Omnipotent as God,
Is destined to go forth and smite
  With more than Aaron's rod.

Thrice holy spot of Middlebrook!
A Mecca to the heart,
As on thy lowly huts we look,
A Delphian shrine thou art,
And in the camp-fire's ruddy gleam,
Which fancy lights anew,
There bursts a holier heavenlier beam
Than e'er Prometheus drew.

The lowly huts of Middlebrook!
Our fathers rested there;
And green forever be the nook,
And pure that Jersey air;
And may the pillar and the cloud
That went before their host
Still rear its canopy of flame,
Nor by their sons be lost.

—REV. EDWARD L. JONES

GREAT SEAL OF NEW JERSEY

Francis Hopkinson, signer of the Declaration of
Independence, is said to have originated the idea for

the seal of New Jersey, dictating
it to Du Simitiere who drew the
design.

The horse's head was included
because of the prominence of horse
breeding in New Jersey. This is
still true today. Man O' War, one
of the fastest race horses of recent
years, was bred and trained in
Monmouth County, New Jersey.

GREAT SEAL OF
NEW JERSEY

A whole room at the Monmouth County Historical Society is used to display cups he has won, shoes he has worn, and pictures of this fine animal.

The plowshares were included because of the importance of farming, which is to be expected in the seal of the "Garden State."

The two female figures represent liberty and prosperity.

The Great Seal was adopted in 1777 at the Indian King Tavern, Kings Highway, Haddonfield, N. J.

SIGHT–SEERS OFFERING GOOD WISHES TO MAN O' WAR ON HIS
TWENTY–FIRST BIRTHDAY, MARCH 22, 1938

OLD QUEENS, RUTGERS

ON THE BANKS OF THE OLD RARITAN

My father sent me to old Rutgers,
And resolved that I should be a man;
    And so I settled down
    In that noisy college town,
On the banks of the old Raritan.

Chorus:

On the banks of the old Raritan, my boys,
Where old Rutgers evermore shall stand,
    For has she not stood
    Since the time of the flood,
On the banks of the old Raritan.

Then sing aloud to Alma Mater,
And keep the Scarlet in the van;
For with her motto high,
Rutgers' name shall never die,
On the banks of the Old Raritan.

Chorus:

WAMPUM

When the Dutch and Swedes came to the valley of the Delaware, they found the Indians using a form of money which they called *wampum*.

The settlers had little actual coin themselves, and as they dealt a great deal with the Indians, they gradually adopted the use of this shell money. The settlers provided by custom and by law for its use among themselves and with the Indians.

The wampum originally was made from clam shells. It was so formed that it could be strung on a leather thong. The white beads were called *wampum* and the purple beads, *suckhanock* or *black wampum*. The suckhanock was worth twice the value of the wampum.

Some of the settlers set up wampum mints—factories in which they made wampum, just as we have mints to make our currency today. These wampum mints continued to be used even after there were no Indians in New Jersey.

One of these wampum mints was set up by John Campbell before the Revolution at Pascack, now Park Ridge, New Jersey. He brought conch shells from Florida, hauled them by wagon overland to his mint,

and made the wampum from them.   This wampum
was sold to Indian agents and traders in what was then
the far West.   This mint was operated as late as 1860.
Today it is still possible to pick up pieces of wampum
around the ruins of the old mint.

TEMPE WICKE

In the spring of 1780, there was great difficulty in
getting teams enough to remove the army stores or
horses enough for the cavalry.   Horses were needed,
the army was moving from winter quarters.

Mr. Wicke's daughter, Tempe, owned a beautiful
young horse, which she frequently rode, and always
with great skill.   She was an admirable and bold rider.

One day, as the preparations for removing the army
were progressing, Miss Wicke rode her favorite horse

TEMPE WICKE'S HOUSE AT MORRISTOWN

to the house of her brother-in-law, Mr. Liddel, on the road to Mendham.

On her return, she was stopped by some soldiers who commanded her to dismount and give them her horse.   One of them seized the bridle reins.

Tempe remained calm and appeared to submit to her fate, but not without a vain entreaty not to take her pet from her.   She told the soldiers, finally, that she was sorry to part with the animal, but as she must, she would ask two favors of them: one, that they would return the horse to her, should it be found possible;   and second, whether they returned him or not, they would be good to him.

The soldiers agreed and believing she was about to dismount, let go of the bridle reins.   No sooner was the horse released than she touched her whip to the spirited steed and sped away like an arrow.

TEMPE WICKE LEADING HER HORSE INTO THE HOUSE

The disappointed soldiers fired after her, probably without intending to hit her. At any rate she was unharmed.

She urged her horse up the hill, at breakneck speed. Coming around to the kitchen door, Tempe sprang off and led him into the kitchen, from there across the living room into the spare bedroom, which had but one window which was closed by a shutter.

Shortly after Tempe and her horse were securely hidden, the soldiers came up. They searched the barn and the woods in vain, never thinking to look in the house.

Tempe Wicke kept her horse in that bedroom until the last trooper was gone. Some say it was three days, some say it was three weeks before she felt it was safe to bring her pet out of his hiding place.

Tempe saved her horse. You may see the house today, and the room that had such a strange guest, on the Jockey Hollow Road if you go to Morristown.

JOCKEY HOLLOW

The troops marched to the camp on the Jockey Hollow Road to spend the winter of 1779–1780.

It was a second Valley Forge, both as to lack of necessary food and clothing for the troops and because of the general discouragement.

For several weeks that army had been on half allowance, the supplies were exhausted, and there was no money to supply the lack.

The campgrounds were about four miles southwest of the green at Morristown. Two roads led to it: the Jockey Hollow Road and the Basking Ridge Road.

Colonel John Stark's brigade was encamped on the southeast slope of Kemble's Mountain sometimes called Mount Kemble. A monument built of the stones gathered from the ruins of the chimneys of the soldiers' huts now marks the location of the camp on Kemble's Mountain.

A little more than halfway from Morristown Green down the Jockey Hollow Road and on the left in sight of the road, was the camping grounds of Clinton's New York brigade.

Primrose Brook, which crosses the campgrounds, furnished water to the soldiers.

The officers and men were in a pitiful condition. Added to the scarcity of food, was the intense cold. Snow lay from four to six feet deep, and the roads were blocked. A blizzard swept the countryside burying some of the soldiers in their tents like sheep. For ten days, only two pounds of meat for each man was received; then for six or eight days there was no meat; then for six or eight days more, no bread. The desperate soldiers were driven to rob the country people, although, considering the condition in which the army was, little of this was done. The soldiers were so weak from hunger and cold that they were unable to perform military duty or to build their huts. They did not get these huts built and move into them until February.

General Washington spent that winter at the Ford house in Morristown but his experiences were nevertheless severe. Eighteen of his official family were crowded together in the kitchen, hardly one of whom could speak above a whisper because of the colds they had. There was no provision for cooking meals and little to cook.

Money was so scarce that for a time, the paymasters department was unable to send public despatches because they could not pay the postage.

Much of the land on which the camp was located was owned by Henry Wicke, father of Tempe. Some of the officers stayed at his house that winter.

It was during this winter that General Benedict Arnold was court-martialed and convicted as a traitor

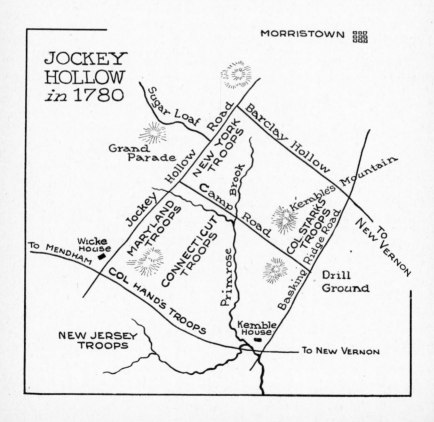

MORRISTOWN

JOCKEY HOLLOW in 1780

Sugar Loaf

Grand Parade

Jockey Hollow

NEW YORK TROOPS

Barclay Hollow

Camp Brook

Camp Road

Kemble's Mountain

COL. STARKS TROOPS

Ridge Road

TO NEW VERNON

MARYLAND TROOPS

CONNECTICUT TROOPS

Primrose

Baskine

Drill Ground

To MENDHAM

Wicke House

COL. HAND'S TROOPS

NEW JERSEY TROOPS

Kemble House

To NEW VERNON

to the cause he had once fought for so bravely. This court-martial was held at the Norris Tavern on Jockey Hollow Road.

With the spring hope revived. On the seventh of June, Washington moved his army to Short Hills or the Heights of Springfield, from there to Whippany, to Preakness, to Paramus, to King's Ferry where he crossed the Hudson, to the Robinson House just below West Point.

On the fourth of July, 1933, Jockey Hollow Camp-grounds including the Tempe Wicke house, Washington's Headquarters (Ford House), and Fort Nonsense were presented to the Federal Government and together form the only national historical park in the United States.

> "Across the old Morris Green they march
>   And take the mountain road
> To their winter quarters mid the hills
>   And there make their abode.
>
> "With beat of drums and flying flags
>   And never-ending tramp
> Of horse and man they pass to reach
>   That bleak midwinter camp."
>
> —C. D. PLATT
> *Ballads of New Jersey in the Revolution*

ROBERT TREAT

In the winter of 1665–1666, some of the inhabitants of Guilford, Branford, and Milford, Connecticut, finding themselves in need of more farming land, sent a committee to report on the land in the neighborhood of Elizabethtown, New Jersey, which was being advertised for settlement by the royal proprietors of that province, Berkeley and Carteret.   Their report was a favorable one.

In May, 1666, with Robert Treat as leader, thirty families purchased the land on which, today, are situated Newark, Springfield, Livingston, Orange, Bloomfield, and Caldwell.   A statue, erected on the

From Painting in Robert Treat Hotel, Newark

THE LANDING OF ROBERT TREAT

two hundred fiftieth anniversary of this purchase at Broad and Bridge Streets, Newark, preserves the story for us in stone.

In return for the land, the Indians received fifty double hands of powder, one hundred bars of lead, twenty axes, twenty coats, ten guns, twenty pistols, ten kettles, ten swords, four blankets, four barrels of beer, ten pairs of breeches, fifty knives, twenty horses, eight hundred fifty fathoms of wampum, six ankers of liquor, and three troopers coats. The whole worth about seven hundred fifty dollars. Today this land,

Migration of Robert Treat and his followers

purchased so cheaply, is worth over five hundred
million dollars.

Robert Treat and his followers settled on the Passaic
River.   They first called their new town Milford,
after Milford, Connecticut, the former home of their
leader.   Later, the name was changed to Newark in
honor of their good and kind minister, Abraham
Pierson, who had been ordained in Newark, England.

Today, Newark is the largest city in New Jersey;
and Robert Treat might well feel proud of the city in
which he is honored as its founder.

ELIZABETH, FOR THE GOVERNOR'S LADY

Elizabeth, or as it was first known, Elizabethtown,
was the seat of the first English Government in
New Jersey.

Nova Caesarea, or New Jersey, was bought in 1664
from the Duke of York, by the Lords Proprietors, John
Lord Berkeley and Sir George Carteret.   It received
its name, New Jersey, because of the fact that Sir
George Carteret had formerly been Governor of the
Isle of Jersey, which lies southeast of England.

Elizabeth seems to have been a name which occurred
frequently in the Carteret family.   This may have
influenced the choice of the name for his new capital.
Or, it might have been the fact that his grandfather
was knighted by Queen Elizabeth.   However, tradition
says that Elizabeth was named for Elizabeth, the
wife of Sir George.   Thus, was named the little
settlement which set itself up as the first capital of
New Jersey.

ON THE ROAD FROM MACAPIN TO BUTLER, PASSAIC COUNTY

"One does not need to be a Jerseyman to admire such a view as he gets from the Short Hills, Eagle Rock, or the rugged ledges of rock just north of the tollgate on the mountain back of Montclair."

HANNAH ARNETT

It was during the dark, discouraging, days of the Revolutionary War that Mrs. Hannah Arnett, of Elizabethtown, heard her husband and several other dispirited patriots discussing the question of giving up the fight for national independence, laying down their arms, and accepting the "protection" of the British.

When she heard them planning to desert the cause they had been fighting for, she burst into the room, and in spite of her husband, rebuked them for their weakness and cowardice.

"What greater cause could there be," said she, "than that of country. I married a good man and true, a faithful friend, and loyal Christian gentleman, but it needs no divorce to sever me from a traitor and a coward. If you take the infamous British protection which a treacherous enemy of your country offers you, you lose your wife, and I—I lose my husband and my home!"

Hannah Arnett's words had the desired effect. Her husband saw what they were planning in its true light as did the others, and stood fast by the cause of America.

THE MAN OF MANY TRADES
THE REVEREND JACOB GREEN

In the early days, only a few places could afford to have a pastor or minister of their own. Several "churches" would be preached to by the same pastor on successive Sundays. Besides this the pastor was required to keep all the records of births, marriages, and deaths in that territory, which was not quite so big a job as it sounds, because the families were fewer and more scattered than they are today. However, the pastor could scarcely be sure of a comfortable living, certainly not enough to feed his usually large family.

Parson Jacob Green at Hanover, Morris County, had just such a "charge" as has been described and just such a family. His salary was small, and he says that this "led him to take more worldly cares and business than he could have chosen." His congregation encouraged him to add to his income by earning money in other ways, assuring him that "country congregations could not have ministers unless ministers would take some care to provide and help support their own families!"

He studied and practiced medicine, he had a school under his care, often wrote and executed wills for his patients, and had a share both in a grist mill and a distillery. He could bring you into the world, baptize you, teach you when you were a child, supply you with flour for your bread, sell you wine for your wedding, marry you, care for you when dying, write your will, and execute it for you after your death. He, probably, had a share in the undertaking business, though there is no record or suspicion of it.

Some one intending to tease the Reverend Green about his "many trades" addressed a letter to him as follows:

"To the Rev. Jacob Green, Preacher
And the Rev. Jacob Green, Teacher;
To the Rev. Jacob Green, Doctor
And the Rev. Jacob Green, Proctor;
To the Rev. Jacob Green, Miller
And the Rev. Jacob Green, Distiller."

Needless to say, he received the letter.

His parsonage is still standing near the Hanover post office.

STONE SOUP

An amusing story is told of a joke played on hot-tempered, kind-hearted General William Winds of the New Jersey Militia, a native of Morris County, in the spring campaign of 1777 somewhere near Woodbridge.

Supplies were scarce, the men were hungry. Two soldiers named Heniman and Camp planned this scheme to work on his sympathies.

The two scamps got a smooth stone, placed it in their camp kettle, and set it to boiling. Soon General Winds came along.

"Well, men, anything to eat?" he inquired.

"Not much, General," they replied, gravely.

"What have you got in the kettle?" said he, coming up to the fire.

"A stone, General, for they say there is some strength in stones, if you can only get it out!"

"There ain't a bit of strength in it. Throw it out. You must have something besides that to eat."

With that, he left and rode rapidly to the farmhouse of a Quaker in the neighborhood. The good man's wife had just baked a batch of bread.

"My friend," said Winds, "my soldiers are starving, and I want that bread."

"Thee cannot have it to help men to fight.   Thee knows it is against the belief of the Friends to aid in warfare," the woman answered.

"I don't care a fig about 'Thee' and 'Thou,' but I want the bread.   Here is the money."

"I cannot take thy money for such purposes."

"Very well," said the General, putting the money back in his pocket, "it will be left to buy something else with, but the bread I will have, money or no money."

With that he placed the loaves of bread in a bag, and throwing it across his horse, carried it back to the camp, where he distributed it, not forgetting the two soldiers who were making stone soup.

GENERAL WINDS OF ROCKAWAY

O have you heard the General pray,
Brave General Winds of Rockaway,
In the Deacon's Meetings that they hold
Where patriots meet, both true and bold?
'Twas there I heard him many a day
Brave General Winds of Rockaway.

In the old unplastered church they met;
No parson was there the text to set;
But when the General once began,
Loud waxed the voice of that valiant man:
Oh yes, I've heard him many a day,
Brave General Winds of Rockaway.

And when at Chatham Bridge he stood
And faced the foe, they thought it good
To take a hint that the General dropped,
So they took to their heels and never stopped;
For he could fight as well as pray,
Brave General Winds of Rockaway.

—CHARLES D. PLATT

From Ballads of New Jersey in the Revolution.

GOD'S ACRE

Here lie the fathers of a day gone by,
   Who toiled in wood, and fields of living green,
And every year that speeds beneath the sky
   Strikes from the landscape some familiar scene.

How quiet was this spot, when girt about
   With paths that wandered here and there at will.
Before the city sent its clamorous shout
   To wake and trouble hearts that would be still.

Men question what you did, and with a laugh
   We reckon up the things to you unknown.
Our children mock the artless epitaph
   Which lingers yet on broken, crumbling stone.

Our thoughtless age would cast your dust away
   And sell God's acre for a pot of gold,
Believing much in self, too wise to pray,
   Believing all things may be bought and sold.

Yon church was built by men of earnest heart,
   Who gave their time and labor to the task,
Who fashioned each distinct and separate part,
   Nor thought their very best too much to ask.

And here are sleeping, men who turned the tide
　When shock of battle threatened all the land,
And now enshrined within their country's pride,
　They challenge us to measure where they stand.

What are we building that will last as long,
　And what, believing that will meet their test?
Will poet find our life a theme for song,
　When skies are growing red within the west?
　　　　　　　—GEORGE ARMSTRONG LIGGETT

"PUT WATTS INTO 'EM, BOYS"

"Here's the spot.   Look around you.　Above on the
　　height
Lay the Hessians encamped.   By that church on the
　　right
Stood the bold Jersey farmers; and here ran a wall—
You may dig anywhere and you'll turn up a ball;
Nothing more.   Grasses spring, waters run, flowers
　　blow,
Pretty much as they did a century ago.

"Nothing more, did I say?   Stay one moment; you've
　　heard
Of Caldwell, the parson, who once preached the Word
Down at Springfield?   What, no?   Come—that's
　　bad; why, he had
All the Jerseys aflame!   And they gave him the name
Of the 'rebel high priest.'   He stuck in their gorge,
For he loved the Lord God—and he hated King
　　George!

"Did he preach? did he pray?   Think of him as you
    stand
By the old church today—think of him and his band
Of military ploughboys!   See the smoke and the heat
Of the reckless advance, of that straggling retreat!

". . . They were left in the lurch
For want of more wadding.   He ran to the church,
Broke down the door, stripped the pews, and dashed
    out in the road
With his arms full of hymn books, and threw down
    his load
At their feet!   Then above all the shouting and shots
Rang his voice, 'Put Watts into 'em!   Boys, give
    'em Watts.'

"And they did.   That is all.   Grasses spring, flowers
    blow
Pretty much as they did ninety-three years ago.
You may dig anywhere and you'll turn up a ball—
But not always a hero like this—and that's all."

Thus Bret Harte tells the story.

Dr. Ashbel Green says his father, Rev. Jacob Green,
witnessed the fight from the adjoining hills.

The Rev. James Caldwell on seeing the need of more
wadding for the guns, did, indeed, fling hymn books
to the soldiers, shouting to them, "Put Watts into
'em, boys."   (They were Watts' hymns.)

While the Americans had fewer men than the British,
they made their enemies pay dearly in killed and
wounded; and at Springfield forced the redcoats to
retreat.

As the British advanced on Springfield, the little village of Connecticut Farms, now Union, at which James Caldwell was pastor, was captured. As the fighting drew nearer, Mrs. Caldwell with her children and a servant girl moved into one of the more sheltered rooms of the parsonage. As Mrs. Caldwell sat on the bed, comforting her baby, a British soldier came to the window and fired at her, killing her instantly.

CHURCH AT SPRINGFIELD

Where the fighting parson tore up the Bibles and hymn books for wadding for the guns at the battle on June 23, 1780.

The town of Connecticut Farms was burned, and it was with difficulty that her body was dragged to the street where it lay in the sun for some while.   Finally, permission was obtained to take her body to a near-by

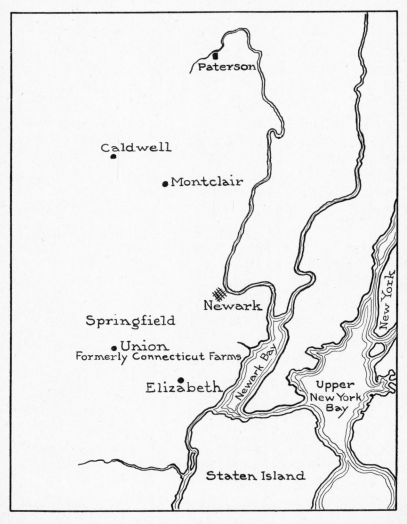

house, that of Captain Henry Wade, one of the few buildings left standing.

While all this was taking place, her husband was with the American Army at Springfield, taking part in the fight and uttering his brave words.

That night, he overheard some soldiers talking about his wife's pitiful fate. You may imagine how he felt! He asked them what they knew, but they would not tell him.

He set out immediately to Connecticut Farms, taking a flag with him, so that he could get through the lines. He could see the town and church, there, in ruins. He found his wife's friends gathered for the funeral in the midst of the surrounding desolation. He arrived in time to take part in the services.

Today, there is a monument at the church at Springfield from which he took the hymn books to give them to the soldiers. There is also a tablet at the bridge, east of the village telling of his part in the battle of Springfield on that twenty-third of June, 1780, erected by the state of New Jersey.

While he was Deputy Quartermaster General of the American Army, and pastor of the First Presbyterian Church of Elizabethtown (Elizabeth), he was shot and killed by an American soldier who had a grudge against him, and who had intended to "pop Caldwell over."

The fighting parson was bitterly mourned throughout New Jersey as a "pious and fervent Christian, the zealous and faithful minister, the eloquent preacher, and prominent leader among the worthies who secured the liberties of his country."

Caldwell, New Jersey, is named for him.

A SOLDIER DOES NOT SURRENDER HIS GUN

One evening, when the soldiers were gathered around the camp fire talking, they began discussing various members of the Company from Denville, and their outstanding characteristics. In the course of the talk, David Garrigus' name was mentioned. He was noted for his steadfastness and sense of duty. If he were told to do a thing, he did it with all his might.

That particular evening, David happened to be on guard duty. Samuel Shongom, who liked a contest of any kind, and particularly, a trial of strength, made a wager with the rest of the group that though David was steadfast in his duty, still he, Samuel Shongom, could take his gun away from him.

Now, one thing a soldier must never do, and that is surrender his gun while on guard duty to any but his superior officers. Samuel and David were both privates.

"Let me see your gun a minute, David," said Samuel.

"You know I cannot do that, neighbor," replied David. For these two were neighbors as well as fellow soldiers.

"Just a minute, nobody will see you. I'll give it right back," Samuel coaxed. The others had concealed themselves so that they might see who should win, and yet not be seen themselves.

"No," was the reply. "I will not give you my gun."

Angered that his friends should see him lose the wager he had so confidently made, Samuel seized David's gun and tried to wrest it from his grasp. Both were strong men, their muscles hardened by long hours of toil on their farms. Back and forth, they struggled, neither gaining over the other. When by some terrible mischance, the gun was discharged. Samuel groaned and crumpled up on the ground.

Horrified at what had happened, David went for help immediately. But Samuel Shongom was beyond help.

Fortunately for David, the other soldiers had seen the whole struggle and, indeed, knew the cause of the contest over the gun, which David did not know. They explained to the captain, who after expressing his regret at what had happened said, "Your country needs all its brave men. Here is one dead, and another deeply saddened through no fault of his own, by what you intended for fun. In the future, try to think of the consequences of such acts before you do them."

Doubtless, for the remainder of their lives, these soldiers were sadder and wiser men.

David Garrigus, his father, and three brothers served with honor in the war.

PULASKI SKYWAY

The Pulaski Skyway in New Jersey is the most expensive road in the world for its length. It is three miles long and fifty feet wide. It can easily accomodate five lanes of traffic and it is estimated that 20,000,000 vehicles use it annually. It resembles a huge bridge over the Hackensack and Passaic Rivers, and the Meadows.   Its cost, including that of the approaches, is $40,000,000.

It was named for Count Casimir Pulaski, who had won fame as commander in chief of the army of Poland. It was his reputation as a soldier that caused Benjamin Franklin to send him to America to join Washington's Army.

In 1778, he was ordered to raise a special troop of cavalry called the *Pulaski Legion*.   The men were selected for their skill in horsemanship and their boldness in fighting.   It was a great honor to belong to this brave band and before long he had three companies of cavalry and three companies of infantry.   Many of the officers of the Pulaski Legion were foreigners like the Count himself, lovers of freedom willing to help a struggling people gain their liberty.   The Legion became famous for its daring and brave deeds and was often chosen by General Washington to do some difficult service.

General Pulaski, as he had the right to be called in the American Army, took part in an engagement with the British at Cooper's Ferry, now Camden, in the latter part of February, 1778.   The British, who were stationed at Philadelphia, were scouring that part of New Jersey directly across the river which included

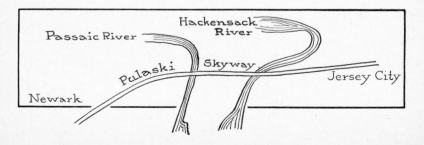

Camden and the surrounding villages. This skirmish took place near what is now Seventh and Market Streets, Camden.

Pulaski was everywhere during the fighting, alert, charging the enemy, and encouraging the soldiers. He had his horse shot under him and he himself captured seven prisoners. General Wayne, sometimes called *Mad Anthony Wayne* because of his own courage and daring, praised Pulaski highly in his report of the battle, saying that the Count had "behaved with his usual bravery."

General Casimir Pulaski took part in engagements with the British at Haddonfield, Egg Harbor, and wintered at Trenton (1777), at Minnisink (1778), and at Morristown (1779).

THE PULASKI SKYWAY

This is New Jersey's famous roadway across the Hackensack and Passaic Rivers. It is the largest viaduct in the world for highway traffic.

He gave $50,000 of his own money, his able services, and finally his life in defense of the liberty of the land of which he said:

"I could not submit to stoop before the sovereigns of Europe, so I came to hazard all for the freedom of America, and am desirous of passing the rest of my life in a country truly free and of settling as a citizen to fight for liberty."

THE WOMEN'S WAY

The courage and endurance of the Morris County women during the Revolution was typical of all New Jersey women during those rugged times.

It was no uncommon thing for these women to cultivate the fields and harvest the crops while the men were away at war. There were only hand tools with the possible exception of a horse-drawn plow or harrow, if the horses had not been taken for the army. It required strong bodies and brave hearts to carry on.

Anna Kitchell was a fair representative of all the Morris County women both in scorning "A British protection" when her husband and four brothers were in the American Army, and in keeping the great pot full of food for the patriot soldiers. She spoke for a thousand like herself when she said so proudly to the Deacon who urged her to get a protection, "If the God of Battles will not take care of us we will fare with the rest!"

The second winter the army was encamped at Morristown the soldiers were repeatedly reduced to the very verge of starvation, with roads blocked with snow for miles, so that at one time a correspondent of a Philadelphia paper says there was "an enforced fast of three days in the camp."

The poor fellows were saved only by their own appeals to the surrounding farmers and by such women as Hannah Carey Thompson, the wife of David Thompson, she that had once scalded a Tory for impudence, and had prepared large kettles of food for the hungry men.

Ladling out the food from the great pot, she said, "Eat away, men; you are welcome because you are fighting for the country; and it is a good cause you are engaged in!"

New Jersey men fought for our country and so did the women!

WASHINGTON'S HEADQUARTERS
AT MORRISTOWN

The dwelling occupied by Washington as his headquarters in the winter of 1779–1780, is situated about half a mile east of the public square, on the Newark and Morristown turnpike, and was the residence then of Colonel Jacob Ford, who commanded the first regiment of Morris County militia during Washington's retreat through the state.

The General and his suite occupied the whole building except the two rooms east of the entry, which were retained by the family. The front room, west of the door, was his dining room, and that east in the second story, his sleeping apartment. There was a small log kitchen attached to the eastern end used by Washington's cook, and also a large log structure at the western end, in which Washington, Hamilton, and Tilghman had their offices. Two sentinels paraded in front of the house and two in the rear constantly, day and night. The life guard, composed of two hundred fifty men, under General William Colfax, were quartered in some fifty rude huts which stood in the meadow formed by the angle of the two roads a few rods southeast of the dwelling.

With the exception of paper and paint, an added partition or two and the filling up of the spacious fireplace for a coal grate, no changes have been made in this famous house since Washington occupied it.

WASHINGTON'S HEADQUARTERS AT MORRISTOWN
General and Mrs. Washington spent the winter of 1779-1780, in this house,
the most famous of Washington's Headquarters.

Much of the furniture was in the house when Washington lived there. "It is no ordinary place."

Count Pulaski frequently exercised his corps of cavalry in front of the headquarters. He was an expert horseman, and performed many feats of skill. He would, sometimes, while his horse was at full gallop, discharge his pistol, toss it in the air, catch it by the barrel, and throw it ahead as if at an enemy. With his horse still on the jump, he would lift one foot out of the stirrup, and, with the other foot in, bend to the ground and recover the weapon. Some of the best horsemen in the army, the Virginia lighthorse, attempted to imitate the feat.   Once in three or four times they could succeed in catching the pistol; none, however, were able to pick it up from the ground, but in their attempts they got some terrible falls.

—BARBER AND HOWE'S *Historical Collection of N. J.*

Adapted

A JERSEY ROMANCE AND TRAGEDY

During Washington's second winter (1779–1780) at Morristown, Elizabeth Schuyler, daughter of General Philip Schuyler, came to the Campfield house there.

Two of General Washington's staff officers had met her at her father's house at Albany, New York, and upon her coming to Morristown, immediately laid siege to her heart.   These two young men were Alexander Hamilton and Tench Tilghman.

It soon became plain that the handsome, young Hamilton was winning.   The romance was the talk of the town and was watched with sympathetic eyes by all the American camp.

The story is told that on one night after calling on Elizabeth, Hamilton was stopped on his way back to camp and asked for the countersign.   He had not the faintest idea what it was, but leaned over and whispered to the sentry, "Tell me."

The sentry recognized the young officer and with a twinkle in his eye, did tell him.

Hamilton drew himself up, gave the countersign, saluted the soldier, and went on his way to his quarters.

Courtships in war time cannot be long.   The young people were married at the Schuyler homestead in Albany, December 14, 1780.

TRUMBULL'S PORTRAIT OF ALEXANDER HAMILTON

The Hamiltons lived happily. Alexander Hamilton did much for his country after the war, as Secretary of the Treasury. In 1795, he retired from public office and took up the practice of the law in New York City.

He became a leader in party politics in New York and in 1804 succeeded in defeating Aaron Burr, whom the Federalists had nominated for governor of that state.

Smarting under this defeat, Burr determined to be revenged on Hamilton.   This he soon accomplished.

SITE OF BURR-HAMILTON DUEL AT WEEHAWKEN

He challenged Hamilton to a duel.   Pistols were chosen. They met at Weehawken, N. J., across the river from New York, on the morning of July 11, 1804.

Hamilton did not fire at his rival.   Burr shot and mortally wounded him. Alexander Hamilton died next day, and the whole nation mourned its most brilliant statesman.

A monument marks the spot where the duel took place at Weehawken.

PEGGY WARNE

At Washington, New Jersey, a monument was erected, in 1915, to Peggy Warne.

"Aunt Peggy" Warne lived and worked during the time of the American Revolution.

In those days, towns were few, neighbors were scattered, and doctors were almost impossible to obtain for illness.

"Aunt Peggy" filled the place of the country doctor for the people for miles around her home, near Broadway, and filled it well. This was especially true while the doctors were away at war. When illness came, someone rode for "Aunt Peggy" Warne.

This courageous woman kept a horse ready at all times, day and night, and went to the sick and suffering through drifting snow and rain storms.

In gratitude for her kindness and "help in time of trouble" the great-grandchildren of many she helped, as well as some of her own great-grandchildren, erected the monument in her honor.

WILLIAM PATERSON AND THE NEW JERSEY PLAN

When the Articles of Confederation proved too weak to hold the newly independent colonies together, a convention of prominent men was called in order to set up a new form of government that would be sufficiently strong to unite the new nation. Among those men was a lawyer from New Brunswick, a graduate of Princeton University, William Paterson.

There was much discussion about how the states should be represented under the Constitution which the convention was preparing. The larger states, headed by Virginia, believed that each state should be represented according to the number of people in it. This would have been a decided advantage over the smaller states. New Jersey, along with the smaller states believed that each should be equally represented. Eventually a compromise was reached. There would be two Houses of Congress: the Senate elected according to the New Jersey plan—an equal number from each state; the House of Representatives—elected according to the Virginia plan—each state represented according to the number of people in that state.

It was, without doubt, due largely to the ardent support of William Paterson that the New Jersey plan was recognized in so organizing the new government.

Later, under the Constitution, William Paterson represented New Jersey in the Senate. Upon the death of William Livingston, the first governor, Paterson was asked to come to Trenton to fill his place.

While he was governor of New Jersey, a plan for establishing an industrial center at the Falls of the Passaic River was presented. It was Alexander Hamilton's belief that the United States would never be really free and independent of Great Britain until we could manufacture goods enough to supply our own needs. And for this purpose, the legislature of the state was asked for an act to establish a town in which to locate these industries. The Falls of the Passaic was chosen as the location because, here, was to be found the finest water power within convenient reach of New York or Philadelphia.

Because of the help given by Governor Paterson in obtaining this act for establishing the town, it was named for him, Paterson.

PASSAIC RIVER FALLS, PATERSON

HOPE

Many religious groups have helped in developing our country and our state. One of these groups is the Moravians or United Brethren.

They settled at Bethlehem, Pennsylvania, but some of them, later, crossed over into New Jersey and purchased a tract of about one thousand acres of land from Samuel Green for the sum of £563 and proceeded to settle there. This Moravian settlement was the town of Hope, Warren County, New Jersey.

The Moravians, a German Protestant sect, are very tolerant of other religions. People of other religious beliefs that come among them are permitted to keep their religion without interference.

The early settlers of Hope were very honest and trusted that others were the same. They did not seem very fortunate in this faith in others because the story goes that they were frequently cheated. Perhaps this was the cause, or there may have been some other reason, but after remaining at Hope for about thirty-five years, the Moravians began to sell their property and return to Bethlehem.

An interesting custom of the Moravians is their use of the "lot" or lottery to decide various questions of church government and related matters. Even today, if a girl of the Moravian faith cannot make up her mind whether she will accept a suitor, she may ask that the lot be cast. Then according to the lottery her answer is given.

Churches of this religion exist in various parts of New Jersey.   Their interest or importance is not confined to this one town, Hope, nor to New Jersey. Something of their story is told here because to New Jersey, the Moravians gave Hope.

THE MORAVIAN NUNS AT BETHLEHEM, PA., MADE AND PRESENTED THIS BANNER TO GENERAL PULASKI AND HIS LEGION.

THE MINISINK REGION

This region has had an identity of its own not only for years but for centuries. The name itself tells its story.

The Minsies or the "lands from which the waters have gone" are said to have been formerly the bottom of a lake that covered this section. When the river broke through at the present Delaware Water Gap, the lake was drained, leaving fertile lands.

This region was inhabited by a tribe of Lenni-Lenape Indians, known as Minsies. They had the wolf for their totem or coat-of-arms. The Minisink Region, as this region has been known for many years, had a place in the religion of the Lenni-Lenapes. They believed that this land was a direct gift from the Great Spirit to them, as the first or original people. The river was known in their language as the "river of the original people." Their council hall was on the level plateau near Milford, Pennsylvania, called by the settlers *Powwow Hill.*

The Minisink Region is not by any means confined to New Jersey, but extends for about forty miles on both sides of the Delaware and Neversink Rivers, northward from Delaware Water Gap. It includes much of Orange County, New York, as well as much of Sussex County, New Jersey. We find the name in Minisink Island, Minisink Creek (or Westbrook) in Sussex County, New Jersey; Minisink Township, and Minisink Post Office in Orange County, New York;

"MINISINK"

and another Minisink east of Lake Hopatcong in Morris County, New Jersey.

The first Europeans to settle in this region came from the direction of the Hudson, following down the tributary river valleys to the Neversink and Delaware Rivers when they settled. They bought their land from the Indians, as did the English when they came up the Delaware Valley. It is probable that the payment was of the usual sort: rum, beads, guns, and bright colored cloth.

The Indians, feeling as they did about their land, believed that, though it was a gift of the Great Spirit to them, it was for the use of all mankind. When they realized that the white man looked on the land as valuable property for which he paid in almost worthless goods, they deeply resented such payment and the Indian attacks and "outrages" began. But it took that famous piece of trickery, the "Walking Purchase," to arouse the Lenni-Lenapes thoroughly. This was perpetrated by the agents for the Colony of Pennsylvania. The purchase was intended by the Indians to include the land only to the Lehigh River Valley. By unfair means, the agreement was made to include the land of the Minsies on the west side of the Delaware River.

There were two "Walking Purchases," although the second is the more famous or rather infamous of the two. The first was made between William Penn and the Indians, when Penn bought as far as could be walked in a day, according to Indian custom, stopping to rest and smoke and walking till sundown. This purchase included the land to a point about opposite the present city of Trenton, New Jersey. More land was needed, presently, and a second "Walking Purchase" was arranged between Penn's agents and the Indians. The white men advertised for men who had great endurance and speed. When the "walk" began, these men were supplied with a horse carrying food and rum before them. They traveled fast and did not stop to rest and smoke with the Indians, as was the custom, but traveled continuously as fast as their legs would carry them. When the party had passed the Lehigh River, the place which the Indians had intended to be the boundary, the red men realized what was happening—that the land of the Minsies would be included in the purchase, and shortly after they left the group and fled to warn their villages that the land was theirs no more.

The claim is made that, had the Indians lost this land in fair fight, they would have considered it as an indication of the will of the Great Spirit; but to be cheated out of it was another matter. Indian attacks became more and more frequent. Swartswood Lake in Sussex County is named for the Swartwout family, victims of one of these Indian raids.

At the time of the French and Indian War, this feeling was fanned into flame by the French for their own purposes. Teedyuscung, an Indian chief, led the Indians against the white settlers until Governor Denny of Pennsylvania sent for him and peace for a time was restored.

Homes of people who had cheated the Indians or who had had some part in action against them were attacked, burned, and the inhabitants murdered. The

Indians were regarded as were the other wild beasts of the forest. Indian hunts were organized, just as deer hunts are today, except that there was no closed season on Indians.

But actual war once more broke out when the British made allies of the Lenni-Lenapes against the Americans. A chief, Thayendanega, better known by his English name and rank as Colonel Joseph Brant, a full-blooded Indian with a college education and Christian training, led his countrymen against the white settlements. An expedition formed of men from Goshen, New York, and Sussex County, New Jersey, went out against Brant and his Indians with the idea of preventing the redskins from attacking their homes. The Americans were defeated and their bones left to bleach where they fell in what is known as the Battle of Minisink. This was fought near the mouth of Lackawaxen Creek, in Orange County, New York. It is claimed that during this battle, when Brant had his tomahawk raised to strike, the American who was menaced gave him the Masonic sign. Brant, being a Free Mason, did not tomahawk him but showed him the way to safety. Of 149 men, only 30 of the Americans returned. The Indians had laid waste homes, and had murdered many of the settlers.

The American Generals, Clinton and Sullivan, were sent by General Washington to teach the Indians a lesson. They completely destroyed their strength and never afterwards did the red men revenge themselves on the white owners of the Minisink.

MOODY'S ROCK

The crags, caves, and rocky fastnesses of Sussex County abound with tales of Tories, outlaws, and robbers.

One of the most famous of these, Moody's Rock, was named for Lieutenant James Moody, a soldier in His Britannic Majesty's army, one of whose hiding places it is said to have been.

His superior officer, General Skinner, whose name was infamous to the struggling Americans in New Jersey, describes his deeds in the following words:

"I do hereby certify that Mr. James Moody came within the British lines in April, 1777, and brought with him upwards of seventy men, all of whom, except four, entered into my brigade; that in June following he was sent into the rebel country for the purpose of enlisting men for His Majesty's services, with orders to continue there until a favorable opportunity offered for him to disarm the rebels and arm the loyalists, and with what men he could collect, to join the royal army, but he was prevented from putting this plan into execution by our (the royal army) army's taking a different route from what was expected; that Mr. Moody, being thus disappointed, assisted by two of his neighbors, soon after embodied about one hundred men, with whom he attempted to join the British army, but was unsuccessful; that afterwards he made two successful excursions into the rebel country, and brought with him from Sussex County about sixty able-bodied recruits, nearly all of whom entered into my brigade; that after this time he made many trips into New Jersey and Pennsylvania, and brought with him many good men, and gained many articles of important intelligence concerning the movements of Col. Butler, the real state of the rebel country, the situation and condition of the rebel armies under command of their generals, Washington, Sullivan, etc.; and that while Mr. Moody was under my immediate direction he also destroyed a considerable magazine of stores near Black Point, taking prisoners two colonels, one major, and several other officers, and broke open the Sussex County jail, rescuing a number of loyalists that were imprisoned in it, one of whom was under sentence of death; besides performing many other services.

"I also certify that in the month of October, 1777, the said Moody was mustered as an ensign, but received no pay as such until April, 1778; that he continued his exertions under my directions till 1780, about which time he was taken from the regiment, which prevented his being appointed to a company in it, as it was in general believed the commander in chief intended doing something better for him; that I have every reason to believe Mr. Moody received nothing from government to reward him for his extraordinary services (to the King), or to indemnify him for his extraordinary expenses, till 1780; that from the time of his joining the army, in April, 1777, till his departure for Europe, in May, 1782, he did upon every occasion exert himself with the utmost zeal in support of His Majesty's cause in America; and, on the whole, that I believe all that is related in his printed narrative to be true, without exaggeration. London, January 30, 1783.

"Cortland Skinner
"Brig.-General, &c."

For his daring in capturing dispatches sent to Washington in the spring of 1781, Moody was made a lieutenant.

He plotted, together with his brother and others, to rob the Archives of Congress in Philadelphia in the

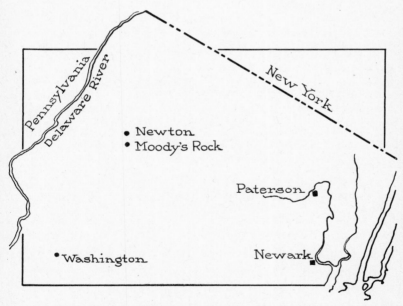

James Moody lived at Newton, though it is said he was not a native of Sussex County.   Moody's Rock is two miles south of Newton in the region of Big and Little Muckshaw.

same year but was betrayed by Addison, a fellow conspirator. His brother was captured and later executed. James Moody, however, finally managed to get away, after many narrow escapes, by hiding in a corn shock which he had watched being searched from a previous hiding place. He hid there two days and two nights without food or drink. When he left the corn shock, he headed for the Delaware River, where he found a boat. He rowed up the river, fell in with some friendly loyalists who helped him to get to New York. Sir Henry Clinton invited him to England. He went in May, 1782. Here, Lieutenant Moody wrote his *Narrative* which was published in London in 1783.

DIARY OF A CONTINENTAL SOLDIER

This is the diary of Timothy Tuttle, a soldier in the first regiment enlisted in New Jersey for the Continental Army in the Revolutionary War. Of course, it is not possible to include all of it. Some of the spelling had to be changed, but there have been as few changes made as possible.

By a call of Congress, made October 9, 1775, New Jersey was to raise two battalions to serve one year, and they were raised accordingly. Of the First Battalion Lord Stirling was Colonel; General Winds, Lieutenant Colonel; and William DeHart, Major. On November 10, 1775, these New Jersey soldiers, six companies of them, were ordered into barracks in New York. The following entries in the diary are of the first two months:

"New Jersey—Journal of Timothy Tuttle, Sergeant, 1st N. J. Regiment, '75 and '76:

Dec. 21st, 1775.
> Saturday, nothing done.
> Monday, went to Brigade.
> Wednesday, stood sentry, and at night.
> Got out at the window, but soon got taken up.
> Saturday, met at 9 and at 4 o'clock for roll call.

31st day, Sabbath, last day of the month.

January 1st, 1776, New Year's Day.   Met at the parade at 9 and at 4, went to church, and an odd crowd at worship that never was to church before.

2nd day.   Met at the parade, and again met and see the mulatto whipped and drummed out of the regiment for stealing.

3rd day.   Met at the parade and good laws were read by Mr. Lord that every one found at a tavern after sunset should be tried at a court martial.   Myself was one of the guard the 1st night that went round the town at sunset and at nine o'clock nobody found.

4th day.   Met at 9 o'clock and not allowed to go to dinner.   4 men whipped this day, 15 lashes each.

5th day.   Met at 9 o'clock and at 4 o'clock. Same night went round the town 3 times on picket guard.   Very muddy.

6th day.   Met at 9 and at 4.

7th day.   Sabbath.   Sergeant Chapan put under guard and 5 our men put in the dark hole but soon got out; beat the door to pieces.

8th day.   Met at the barracks at 9, paraded at the marching ground.

9th day.   Met at 9 o'clock and stood guard that day.

10th day.   Went with a company of 30 men to Baker's in Rahway and for what I can't tell.

11th day.   Met at 9 and at 10 o'clock and ½ after 2, and received by Master same day. Porrage for dinner.

12th day.   Met at parade at 9 and 10 o'clock. Paraded till ½ after 12, then stood sentry at Headquarters 2 hours.

13th day.   Paraded at 10; afternoon got a furlough to go home for 2 days.

14th Sabbath.   Went to Mr. Green's meeting. Fine Discourse.   (Rev. Jacob Green.)

15th day.   This day at home at my father's.

16th day.   Came to Elizabeth town, marched along Stratan's Island after Tories and very muddy.

18th day.   Marched from Bargin Town to N. York to Place nigh Hell Gate at Natty Merson's.

19th day.   Marched from Hell Gate on Long Island to Newtown and from thence to Jamaica at Jis Roberson.

20th day.   Marched from Jamaica on Pursuit of Tories to Rockaway; lodged at Sall Martin's called a Tory.

21st day.   Marched from Rockaway to Captain Hallit's along South side of the Island; Same day, Sabbath our men killed Turkeys and geese and ducks, one hog.

22nd day.   Marched from Captain Hallit's to Hemstead Plains, lodged at Benjamin Hall's; Our men destroyed 2 hives of bees, and behaved very bad on the road to Hempstead.

23rd day.   Marched from Hempstead to Jamaica, lodged at Plat. Smith's same night.

24th day.   Marched from Jamaica to Hell Gate; lodged at a house called Free Mason Lodge.

25th day.   Marched from Hell Gate to New York, and from there to Straton's Island (Staten Island) by water; lodged at Duffy's, I believe a Tory.

26th day.   Marched from Duffy's in Straton's Island to Elizabethtown.

27th day.   Met at parade at 9 and at 4.

28th day.   Sabbath.   Paraded at 9.   Went to meeting (church). Sermon VI Chapter, Exodus; afternoon XL Chapter Isaiah, 6, 7, and 8 verses.

29th day.   Stood sentry at the point for the ship that has been lately taken; Lieutenant Brown 1st man that boarded her, Lord Stirling 2nd man.

30th day.   Came from point at 12 o'clock; Same day some snow.

31st day.   Met at the parade at 9 and at 4.

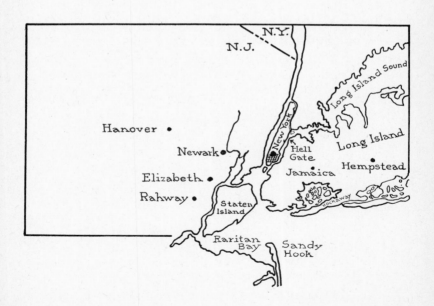

ROCKS THAT LOOK LIKE TREES

Hudson County, in which the greater part of the Palisades are located, is named for one of New Jersey's early discoverers. An Italian, Giovanni da Verrazano, entered New York Bay in 1524. In 1525, a Portuguese sailor, Estavan Gomez arrived. In 1609, Henry Hudson sailed into New York Harbor and up the river which bears his name and which forms the eastern boundary of Hudson County, New Jersey.

Hudson and his men probably were the first Europeans to view the famous Palisades which the Indians called "We-awken" "the rocks that look like trees."

These rocks reach a height of five hundred forty feet near the New York State line and gradually slope south through Bergen County from there to the town of Weehawken where their height is about three hundred feet.

The Palisades are the easternmost of the trap rock ridges extending northwest from the Hudson River near New York City. The Watchung Mountains near Montclair are part of this ridge. This trap rock was used for building stone for many years, furnishing many of the "brown stone fronts" of houses in New York and Philadelphia. Today, the beauty of the Palisades Ridge is valued above its use as building stone although there are quarries in use in other ridges.

The Palisades have been set aside as the Palisades Interstate Park by the states of New Jersey and New York. It extends along the Hudson River from Fort

Lee, New Jersey, to Cornwall-on-the-Hudson, New York. Visit it. It is maintained for your pleasure.

UPPER REACHES OF PALISADES INTERSTATE PARK, OWNED BY NEW YORK AND NEW JERSEY

IRON IN NEW JERSEY

Before the iron mines in Pennsylvania were discovered, New Jersey held an important place as a producer of iron. A considerable amount of iron is still mined in northern New Jersey but the Garden State's importance in iron production has dwindled.

New Jersey has iron ore of two different types: one was deposited in rocks many, many years ago in molten form; the other type is bog iron ore; its name tells where it is found. In some marshes and swampy places or bogs, there are "iron bacteria" in the water. These bacteria take in the iron mixed with other substances and then deposit the iron in the form in which it is found on the floor of the bogs.

During the Revolutionary War and the War of 1812, cannon and shot were made from bog iron ore as well as from the other type. Considerable amounts of bog iron are found in the lakes and swamps of southern New Jersey. Some of the lakes here are not true lakes at all, but are old bog iron mines which have filled with water. After the mines in Pennsylvania were opened, this iron was little used, and as a result furnaces have been abandoned and the homes and villages of the workers stand as lonely reminders of a once prospering industry.

In the rocks of the hills and mountains of northern New Jersey another kind of iron is found. Some of the mines are still in operation, although a number are now closed. One ancient furnace which was supplied with iron from these mines is Ringwood Furnace in Passaic County. This furnace, the Manor House, and grounds were recently presented to the state by Mr. Erskine Hewitt as a museum and monument to commemorate its important part in the Revolutionary War. The grounds are open to the public.

Iron has been forged at Ringwood since about 1739. Cannon, cannon balls, bar iron, and various iron supplies were made here for the American Army in the War of the Revolution. The great iron chain which was stretched across the Hudson at West Point, in order to prevent the British from sailing north of that fort, was forged at Ringwood Furnace. Link by link, it was carried on muleback to West Point, where it was welded together and floated across the river on logs. Part of this chain has been brought back to Ringwood where it may be seen today. Even on the ocean Ringwood had a part, one of the main guns of the good ship "Constitution," better known as "Old Ironsides," which is still preserved and docked in Boston Harbor, was forged at Ringwood Furnace.

Why haven't you read of Ringwood before? General Robert Erskine was the Manager of the Furnace during the Revolution. A British officer, prisoner of war, was paroled in his charge. They became quite friendly. In the course of many conversations, this officer was able to obtain some important information from Erskine and succeeded in getting this to the British forces. Because of this, General Washington ordered that General Erskine's name and the name of Ringwood should not be mentioned in any reports or dispatches. It is believed today that many of the letters written by General Washington and marked "Headquarters," were written at Ringwood, because among the other things which Ringwood can rightfully claim is that the Great General lived here for some time. Washington was staying at Ringwood when Major John André was captured and executed.

The "Forgotten General," Robert Erskine, died and was buried at the ancient cemetery at Ringwood. The elm tree which General Washington planted beside General Erskine's grave was green and flourishing until a few years ago, when it died. Part of the trunk of this tree is preserved in the cellar of Ringwood Manor.

The surrounding country near Ringwood is among the most beautiful in the state. You will feel well repaid should you visit Ringwood.

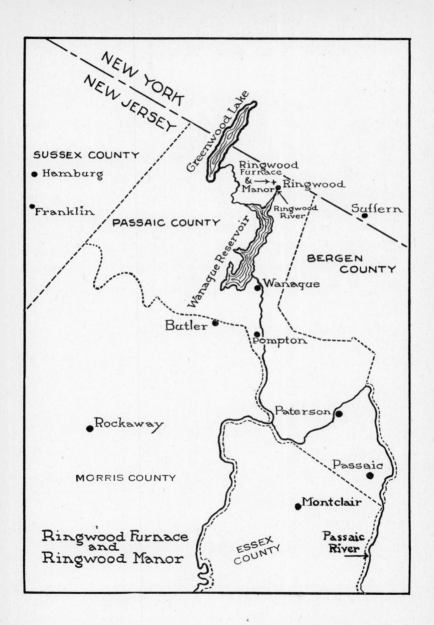

Ringwood Furnace
and
Ringwood Manor

ROCKINGHAM

Washington was quartered at the Judge John Berrien House from August 23 to November 10, 1783.

Here he wrote his Farewell Address to the Army. After the signing of the peace treaty ending the Revolutionary War, he retired to his home at Mount Vernon, Virginia.

Rockingham, as the Berrien House is known, has been made a state shrine to the memory of the Father of Our Country. It is open to visitors.

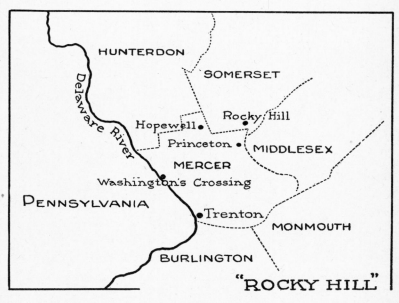

"ROCKY HILL"

WASHINGTON'S HEADQUARTERS, ROCKY HILL, FRONT VIEW

WASHINGTON'S HEADQUARTERS, ROCKY HILL, REAR VIEW
SHOWING SLAVE QUARTERS, AT LOWER LEFT

MAJOR JOHN ANDRÉ

Major André's fame is greatest as the British officer who entered the American lines on his way to New York, after conferring with Benedict Arnold near Stony Point. General Arnold had arranged to turn the American fort at West Point over to the British and then to desert to them. Major André was carrying the plans and information necessary for this transfer to take place. He had disguised himself in order to pass through the American lines to rejoin his troops in New York.

André was stopped by three American soldiers near Tarrytown, New York, searched, and discovered to be carrying these papers. In spite of the bribes he offered them, he was taken to General Washington, who turned him over to the Court Martial. He was tried and found guilty of entering the American lines in disguise carrying valuable information that was harmful to the American cause. He was sentenced to be hanged. This sentence was carried out at Tappan, New York, on October 2, 1780. He was buried in Westminster Abbey, London, England. (When Arnold heard of André's capture, he deserted to the British immediately, an action he lived to regret.)

Major André must have been a likeable, witty, pleasant sort of person from all accounts—an officer and a gentleman. It was unfortunate that he was in disguise when discovered, otherwise it is possible that his exchange might have been arranged. As the conditions existed, there was only one possible course to follow: a sentence of death.

The following poem was written by him. It shows plainly the way the American Army was looked upon by the British forces. It tells its own story. The occasion which is used as the subject of the verses was this: Washington had received information that there were cattle to be had at Bergen Neck, New Jersey, not far from the enemy's lines. The army needed fresh food, and General Anthony Wayne was detailed to get the cattle and at the same time to attack a blockhouse which stood along the Hudson River about half a mile below Bull's Ferry and in the present Hudson County. André gave the last part of the poem to the printer, Rivington, before he left New York on his fatal mission. The poem appeared in the *Royal Gazette* on the morning of the day he was captured. The last stanza, as events took place, is almost prophetic. Some of the poem has been omitted, as it is quite long; the story told in the following verses, however, is fairly complete:

THE COW CHASE

To drive the kine one summer's morn
    The tanner took his way;
The calf shall rue that is unborn
    The jumbling of that day.

And Wayne descending steers shall know,
    And tauntingly deride,
And call to mind in every low
    The tanning of his hide.

Yet Bergen cows still ruminate
Unconscious in the stall,
What mighty means were used to get
And lose them after all.

For many heroes bold and brave,
From New Bridge and Tapaan,
And those that drink Passaick's wave,
And those that eat soupaan;

And sons of distant Delaware,
And still remoter Shannon,
And Major Lee with horses rare,
And Proctor with his cannon:

All wonderous proud in arms they came
What hero could refuse?
To tread the rugged path to fame
Who had a pair of shoes.

At six the Host with sweating buff,
Arrived at Freedom's Pole (Englewood),
When Wayne who thought he'd time enough
Thus specified the whole.

O ye whom glory doth unite,
Who Freedom's cause espouse,
Whether the wing that's doomed to flight
Or that to drive the Cows,

Ere yet you tempt your further way
Or into action Come,
Hear soldiers what I have to say
And take a pint of Rum.

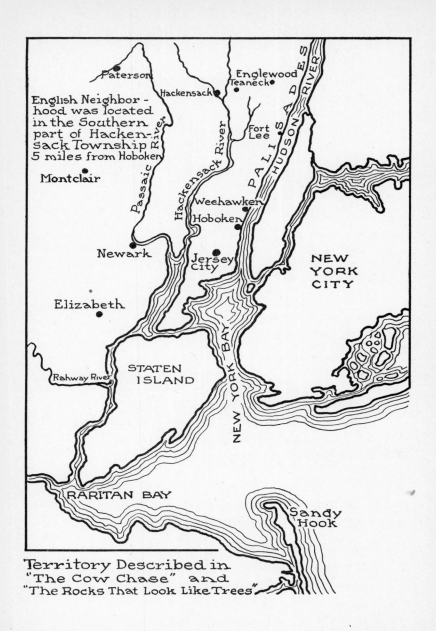

Paterson

English Neighbor-
hood was located
in the Southern
part of Hacken-
sack Township
5 miles from Hoboken

Hackensack

Englewood
Teaneck

Montclair

Fort
Lee

PALISADES

HUDSON RIVER

Passaic River

Hackensack River

Weehawken

Hoboken

Newark

Jersey
City

NEW
YORK
CITY

Elizabeth

Rahway River

STATEN
ISLAND

NEW YORK BAY

RARITAN BAY

Sandy
Hook

Territory Described in
"The Cow Chase" and
"The Rocks That Look Like Trees"

Intemp'rate valor then will string
    Each nervous arm the better,
So all the land shall I O sing
    And read the Gen'ral's letter.

I, under cover of th' attack,
    Whilst you are all at blows,
From English Neighborhood and Tinack
        (Teaneck),
    Will drive away the cows.

For you well know the latter is
    The serious operation,
And fighting with the Refugees
    Is only demonstration.

At Irvine's nod 'twas fine to see
    The left prepare to fight,
While the drovers, Wayne and Lee,
    Drew off upon the right.

In Valor's Phrenzy Hamilton
    Rode like a Soldier Big,
And Secretary Harrison,
    With Pen stuck in his Wig.

But lest the Chieftain Washington
    Should morn them in the Mumps
The fate of Witherington to shun
    They fought behind the Stumps.

Sublime upon his stirrups rose
    The mighty Lee behind,
And drove the terror-smitten cows
    Like chaff before the wind.

But sudden see the woods above
    Pour down another corps;
All helter-skelter in a drove,
    Like that I sung before.

Irvine and terror in the van
    Came flying all abroad;
And cannon, colors, horse, and man,
    Ran tumbling to the road.

Poor Parson Caldwell all in wonder,
    Saw the returning train,
And mourned to Wayne the lack of plunder,
    For them to steal again.

In his dismay, the frantic priest
    Began to grow prophetic;
You'd swore, to see his lab'ring breast,
    He'd taken an emetic.

This solemn prophecy, of course,
    Gave all much consolation,
Except to Wayne, who lost his horse
    Upon the great occasion.

His horse that carried all his prog,
    His military speeches,
His cornstalk—whiskey for his grog,
    Blue stockings and brown breeches.

And now I've closed my epic strain,
    I tremble as I show it,
Lest this same warrior-drover, Wayne,
    Should ever catch the poet.

A BLACKSMITH SHOP OF EARLY DAYS

OLD BLACKSMITH SHOPS OF NEW JERSEY

Only a few years ago every important crossroads in New Jersey had its smithy and wheelwright shop, to which farmers from miles around brought their horses to be shod and their wagons to be repaired.

The steady rhythm of their anvils could be heard and the glow of their forges could be seen as they toiled "week in, week out, from morn till night."

Indeed, Longfellow might have been thinking of a typical Jersey blacksmith when he wrote this poem:

11

Under a spreading chestnut tree
   The village smithy stands;
The smith, a mighty man is he,
   With large and sinewy hands;
And the muscles of his brawny arms
   Are strong as iron bands.

His hair is crisp, and black and long,
   His face is like the tan;
His brow is wet with honest sweat,
   He earns whate'er he can,
And looks the whole world in the face,
   For he owes not any man.

Week in, week out, from morn till night,
   You can hear his bellows blow;
You can hear him swing his heavy sledge,
   With measured beat and slow,
Like a sexton ringing the village bell.
   When the evening sun is low.

And the children coming home from school
   Look in at the open door;
They love to see the flaming forge,
   And hear the bellows roar,
And catch the burning sparks that fly
   Like chaff from a threshing-floor.

He goes on Sunday to the church,
   And sits among his boys;
He hears the parson pray and preach,
   He hears his daughter's voice,
Singing in the village choir,
   And it makes his heart rejoice.

It sounds to him like her mother's voice,
   Singing in Paradise!
He needs must think of her once more
   How in the grave she lies;
And with his hard, rough hand he wipes
   A tear out of his eyes.

Toiling—rejoicing—sorrowing,
   Onward through life he goes;
Each morning sees some task begin,
   Each evening sees it close;
Something attempted, something done,
   Has earned a night's repose.

Thanks, thanks to thee, my worthy friend,
   For the lesson thou hast taught!
Thus at the flaming forge of life
   Our fortunes must be wrought;
Thus on its sounding anvil shaped
   Each burning deed and thought.
           —HENRY WADSWORTH LONGFELLOW

CAMDEN'S GOOD GRAY POET

Walt Whitman was born in West Hills, Suffolk County, Long Island, New York, in 1819.

He was, in turn, a farmer, printer, builder, and author. During the Civil War, he served as a volunteer nurse in the army hospitals until his own health failed. After the war, he worked in a government office. In 1873, he was stricken with paralysis. This forced him to give up his position.

He moved to Camden, New Jersey. Here, he continued to write whenever his health permitted.

WALT WHITMAN HOUSE,
CAMDEN, TODAY

When he died in 1892, he was buried in a fine brown stone tomb in Harleigh Cemetery in that city.

His home at 330 Mickle Street, Camden, is preserved today as a place of interest in his memory.

His ability to see beauty in everyday things is one of the most beautiful points about his poetry.

Here is one of his poems that he wrote while he lived in Camden that shows this quality in him.

The railroad can be seen plainly from his house. You can see it today although the tracks are elevated now. As you read this poem, can you not picture the interested old man at his window looking out into the night and writing down his thoughts?

TO A LOCOMOTIVE IN WINTER

Thee for my recitative,
Thee in the driving storm even as now, the snow, the
    winter-day declining,
Thee in thy panoply, thy measur'd dual throbbing and
    thy beat convulsive,
Thy black cylindric body, golden brass and silvery
    steel,
Thy ponderous side-bars, parallel and connecting rods,
    gyrating, shuttling at thy sides,
Thy metrical, now swelling pant and roar, now taper-
    ing in the distance,
Thy great protruding head-light fix'd in front,
Thy long, pale, floating vapor-pennants, tinged with
    delicate purple,
The dense and murky clouds out-belching from thy
    smoke-stack,
Thy knitted frame, thy springs and valves, the trem-
    ulous twinkle of thy wheels,
Thy train of cars behind, obedient, merrily following,
Through gale or calm, now swift, now slack, yet
    steadily careering;
Type of the modern—emblem of motion and power—
    pulse of the continent,
For once come to serve the Muse and merge in verse,
    even as here I see thee,

With storm and buffeting gusts of wind and falling
    snow,
By day thy warning ringing bell to sound its notes,
By night thy silent signal lamps to swing.

Fierce-throated beauty!
Roll through my chant with all thy lawless music, thy
    swinging lamps at night.
Thy madly-whistled laughter, echoing, rumbling like
    an earthquake, rousing all,
Law of thyself complete, thine own track firmly
    holding,
(No sweetness debonair of tearful harp or glib piano
    thine,)
Thy trills of shrieks by rocks and hills return'd,
Launch'd o'er the prairies wide, across the lakes,
To the free skies unpent and glad and strong.

                              —WALT WHITMAN (1876)

A HOUSE IN CAMDEN

(Corner of Third and Mickle Streets)

Alone, amid the environs of a modern, cheap and
   squalid quarter
Of a quaint old city on the Delaware,
It stands among its neighbors, still, and proud, and
   dignified;
An air from past associations clinging to it still;
A gentlewoman in a dirty crowded thoroughfare.

One feels that haunting sense of former days,
Such a strong air of old associations stays
About it; in the very look of settled permanence that
   speaks
From all its walls of weathered brick a past untold
As rich in story as its tints in gold,
When autumn sunshine through the poplar trees
Makes dancing shadows on the western wall
And lingers lovingly around the quiet door
That seems to offer to a weary foot
Its kindly threshold for a place to rest
And muse, in silence, upon days like these.
Its cold and quiet northern front presents
But shuttered windows; seldom-opened door,
Meant for occasions of solemnity—
A stately wedding or a funeral.
No doubt, in years before,
All of Life's strange processions, grim or gay,
Have passed through, trooping to eternity.

O dear old house, thou proud patrician of a generation
    gone!
Standing aloof, elbowed by foreign neighbors,
Yet in every line
Of ancient weathered walls, retaining still
That settled air of peace and permanence
Not dreamed of in man's habitat today—
The garish flat abode of modern life
That loses meaning as it changes hands;
New desecrations, new monstrosities,
Of fashion or of fancy on array
Lined up in sameness upon every street,
No longer eloquent of Family,
But only human hives to shelter souls,
Flotsam and jetsam of society.

O dear old house; you mean to me one thing
That man to-day has somehow sought in vain,
In eager greed to live, to grasp, to gain
Mere pleasures; thou art a home,
Man's castle, his abode, his place of privacy,
Where, drawn within, away from sordid care,
And contact with the outer world, he may
Sit and commune, surrounded by
His sacred Lares and Penates there,
And musing, know that only he is blest
Who for himself and his a home was wrest
From Life's dispensed gifts to hold possess't.

—Mabel Brown

A FEATHERED HERO

This is "President Wilson," a famous veteran of the World War. Back in 1918 he was a powerful young bird of wonderful vitality, and a very speedy flyer. He was attached to the Tank Corps in France. One gray, foggy morning, during intense machine gun and artillery action, he was released at Grand Pré with a very important message. Twenty-five minutes later he reached his home station, 40 kilometers away, and

"PRESIDENT WILSON"
World War hero, now in the Smithsonian Institution.
(178)

delivered his message safely; but one leg had been shot away and a machine-gun bullet had pierced his breast. After the war "President Wilson" and two other pigeons who had given great service in France were taken to Fort Monmouth, N. J., where they lived with the young carrier pigeons who were being trained by the Army Signal Corps.

—*The Junior Red Cross Magazine*

NEW JERSEY

For I love the State of New Jersey
It's the State where I was born.
It's the land of violets and roses
And of dewy summer morns.
You hear them sing of Tennessee
And dear old Alabam'—
But God made little Jersey
Just another fairyland!
For I love the State of New Jersey
It's the State where I was born!

—ANONYMOUS

BIBLIOGRAPHY

American Literature, by Reuben Post Halleck, M.A., American Book Company, 1911.

Appleton's *New Practical Encyclopedia*, published by D. Appleton & Company, 1910, Vols. 2, 3.

Atlas, Carey's American, published by Matthew Carey, Philadelphia, 1795.

Atlas of World, Cram's Comprehensive.

Barton, Clara, Humanitarian, by Mrs. Corra Bacon Foster, published by Columbia Historical Society, 1918.

Bergen County, History of, by J. M. Van Valen, published by New Jersey Publishing and Engraving Company, New York, 1900. Bowers Printing Co., Philadelphia, 1900.

Bergen and Passaic Counties, History of, New Jersey, by W. Woodford Clayton, assisted by William Nelson, published by Everts & Peck, Philadelphia, 1882. Press by J. B. Lippincott & Company, Philadelphia.

Bonaparte and Bordentown, Letters to the Editor in Philadelphia *Inquirer*, October 8, 1936. Authenticated by J. Tomlinson, President of the Bordentown Historical Society.

Bordentown, Historic Spots of, Pamphlet, 250th Anniversary, October 8–16, 1932. Distributed by Bordentown Historical Society.

Chief American Poets, Edited by Curtis Hidden Page, Ph.D., published by Houghton-Mifflin Company, 1905.

Cleveland, Grover, by George F. Parker, published by Century Company, 1909.

Compton's Pictured Encyclopedia, published by F. E. Compton & Company, 1930, Vol. 9.

Congressional Record, 72d Congress, 1st Session, Remarks of Charles S. Wolverton of New Jersey in the House of Representatives, Washington, D. C., Saturday, July 16, 1932.

Daughters of the American Revolution Magazine, published by the National Society, Daughters of the American Revolution, Washington, D. C., Vol. 67, No. 11; Vol. 68, No. 9.

Encyclopedia Britannica. 11th Edition, Vols. VI, VII, XII, XIII, XIX, XXVIII; 14th Edition, Vol. XIII.

Esso Tours and Detours, published by the Standard Oil Company of New Jersey, August, 1933; September, 1934; June, August, 1935.

Essex and Hudson Counties, New Jersey, History of, Compiled by William H. Shaw, published by Everts & Peck, Philadelphia, 1884. Vol. I.

Franklin, Benjamin, Autobiography of, Edited from manuscript by John Bigelow, published by J. B. Lippincott & Company, Philadelphia, 1868.

Franklin, Benjamin, Memoires De La Vie Privee De, Ecrite par Lui-meme et addresses a son fils; Suivis d'un Precis historique de sa Vie politique et de plusieurs Pieces, relatives a ce Pere de la Liberte a Paris; Chez Buisson, Libraire, rue Hautefeuille, No. 20; 1791. (First Edition of Benjamin Franklin's Autobiography.)

Garrigus-Garrigues *Genealogical Collection.*

Gazetteer, Historical and Statistical, of the State of New York, by French, 1860; by R. P. Smith, publishers.

Gazetteer, Lippincott's New, Edited by Angelo and Louis Heilprin, published by J. B. Lippincott Company, 1906.

Geology, Lectures on Physical and Historical Geology by F. M. Oldach, Ph.D., Professor of Geology at South Jersey Law School, Camden, N. J., 1933.

Geology, Textbook of, by Louis V. Pirsson and Charles Schuchert, published by John Wiley & Sons, Inc., New York, 1929. Vol. I.

Gloucester, Salem, and Cumberland Counties, History of, by Cushing and Shepard, published by Everts & Peck, 1883.

Hancock's Bridge, Official Program of, 150th Anniversary of Skirmish at Quinton's Bridge and Massacre at Hancock's Bridge, May 19, 1928, published by Sunbeam Publishing Company, Salem, N. J.

Hancock House. Address given by Custodian of Hancock House at Daughters of the American Revolution Pilgrimage to Hancock's Bridge, June 14, 1933.

Harte, Bret, Poetical Works of, published by Houghton-Mifflin Company, 1912.

Hudson and Bergen Counties, Genealogical History of, Cornelius Burnham Harvey, Editor, published by New Jersey Genealogical Publishing Company, 114 Fifth Avenue, New York, 1900.

Hunterdon and Somerset Counties, New Jersey, by James P. Snell, published by Everts & Peck, 1881.

Indian Local Names with Their Interpretation, by Stephen G. Boyd, York, Penna., published by the author, 1885. Copyrighted by the author. Inquirer Printing Company, Lancaster, Penna.

Interviews:
J. Tomlinson, President of Bordentown Historical Society.
Thomas J. Rattigan, donor of Clara Barton School, (since deceased).
Mrs. J. Francis Byrns, Regent, Ye Olde Gloucester Chapter, Daughters of the American Revolution.

Junior Red Cross Magazine, published by the Junior American Red Cross, Washington, D. C., November, 1930. (Copyright, American Red Cross.)

Kidd, Captain, Trial of, Edited by Graham Brooks. Made and Printed by William Hodge & Company, Ltd., Glasgow and Edinburgh, September, 1930.

Lighthouses and Lightships of the United States, by George K. Putnam, Houghton-Mifflin Company, 1917.

Makers and Defenders, by Foote and Skinner (Revised), published by the American Book Company, 1929.

Minisink Region, History of, by Charles E. Stickney, published by Coe, Finch, and I. F. Guiwits, Middletown, N. Y., 1867.

Morris County, Centennial Collections of, by Joseph F. Tuttle, D.D. Notation: printer failed before printing was completed. Time: about 1869.

Morris County, History, published by Lewis Historical Publishing Company, 1914. Vol. I.

Morristown, New Jersey, Historic, by Andrew M. Sherman, published by Sherman, Howard Publishing Company, Morristown, N. J., 1905.

National Geographic Magazine, published by National Geographic Society, Washington, D. C., May, 1933. Vol. LXIII, No. 5.

New Jersey, Ballads of, in the Revolution, by C. D. Platt, published by "The Jerseyman Print," Morristown, N. J., 1896.

New Jersey in America, a letter from————, by a Gentleman, late of Christ's College, Cambridge in Pater-Noster-Row, London, 1756.

New Jersey, by Parson, Burgess, and Hulse, published by the New Jersey State Chamber of Commerce, 1928.

New Jersey Colonial Documents, published by the Press Printing and Publishing Company, 1900. Series I and II: Vols. IV, VI, IX, XII, XXII.

New Jersey Colonial Relics, Exhibition at Camden County Historical Society, Camden, N. J.

New Jersey Colonial Relics, owned by Garrigus-Garrigues Family of Morris County.

New Jersey, as a Colony and as a State, by Francis Bazley Lee, published by the Publishing Society of New Jersey, 1902. Vols. I, II.

New Jersey, Common Trees of, by Joseph S. Illick, published by American Tree Association, Washington, D. C., 1927.

New Jersey, Early Forges and Furnaces in New Jersey, by Charles S. Boyer, published by University of Pennsylvania Press, 1931.

New Jersey Gazette, Trenton, May 19, 1779.

New Jersey, History of, by Ellis and Snyder, published by American Book Company, 1910.

New Jersey, Historical Collection of, by Barber and Howe, published for the Authors by S. Tuttle, 194 Chatham Square, New York, 1844.

New Jersey, Historic Roadsides of, published by the Society of Colonial Wars in the State of New Jersey, 1928.

New Jersey, Industrial Opportunities of, by Land-Registry Department of Conservation and Development, State House, Trenton, N. J.

New Jersey, Official Road Map of, State Highway Commissioners, Trenton, N. J., 1930.

New Jersey, People, Resources, and Industries of the Garden State, by J. Russell Smith, published by John C. Winston Company, 1935.

New Jersey, Province of, engraved and published by Wm. Faden, Charing Cross, December 1, 1777. Map.

Official Register of Officers and Men of New Jersey in Revolution, compiled under order of His Excellency, Theodore F. Randolph, Governor, by William S. Stryker, Adjutant General. Printed by the Authority of the Legislature, Trenton, N. J., 1872.

Old Gloucester, Reminiscences of, by Isaac Mickle, published by Townsend Ward & Company, Philadelphia, 1845.

Old Nassau, Abridged Academy Song Book, C. H. Levermore, published by Ginn & Company, 1898.
Old Tennent, A Brochure, by the Trustees, Fourth Edition, Revised, 1931.
Orange County, New York, History of, by Eager, printed by S. T. Callahan, New York, 1846–7.
Pitcher, Molly, Inscription on Monument at Carlisle, Pa.
Primary History, by William H. Mace, published by Rand, McNally & Company, 1909.
Princeton and Its Institutions, by John Frelinghuysen Hagemen, published by J. B. Lippincott & Company, 1878. Vols. I, II.
Pulaski Skyway, Everybody's Column, Philadelphia *Inquirer*, December 31, 1935.
Red Bank, Clipping, Camden *Courier-Post*, May 26, 1936.
Ringwood, Forges and Manor of, from the Notes of Erskine Hewitt, 1932. Pamphlet.
Ringwood, Forges and Manor of, Recollections of Erskine Hewitt, 1935. Pamphlet.
Rockaway Records and Genealogies of Morris County, N. J. Families, by J. Percy Crayon, published by Rockaway Publishing Company, 1902.
Rocky Hill, Washington's Headquarters at, by Mabel Lorenz Ives. Copyrighted by the author, 1932. Published by Lucy Fortune, Upper Montclair, New Jersey.
Ross, Betsy, Clipping, Philadelphia *Evening Bulletin*, Saturday, May 27, 1933. Authenticated by Mrs. J. Francis Byrns, Regent of Ye Olde Gloucester Chapter, Daughters of the American Revolution.
Ross, Betsy, Quaker Rebel, by Edwin S. Parry, published by John C. Winston Company, 1930.
Rutgers University Folder.
Rutgers University Fund Council Bulletin.
Rutgers University Pamphlet.
Salem Oak, Folder distributed by Society of Friends, Salem, N. J.
Salem Oak, Tablet on wall of Friends Cemetery, Salem, N. J.
Somerset County Historical Quarterly, Editor, A. Van Doren Honeyman, Somerset County Historical Society, Publishers, Somerville, N. J. Printed at the office of the Unionist-Gazette Association, Somerville, N. J. Vols. IV, VI.
South Jersey Produces Holly, folder published by the Camden Safe Deposit and Trust Company, Camden, N. J. Vol. II, No. 4.
Story of An Old Farm, by Andrew D. Mellick, Jr., published by *Unionist-Gazette*, Somerville, N. J., 1889.
Stories of Great Americans for Little Americans, by Edward Eggleston, published by the American Book Company, 1895.
Sussex and Warren Counties, New Jersey, by James P. Snell, published by Everts & Peck, 1881. Press by J. B. Lippincott & Company, Philadelphia.
Travels in North America, by Peter Kalm, Professor of Oeconomy in the University of Aobo in Swedish Finland, and Member of the Swedish Royal Academy of Sciences, Translated into English by John Reinhold Forster, F.A.S. Printed by William Eyres, Warrington, 1770. Vols. I, II, III.

Union and Middlesex Counties, New Jersey, History of, by W. Woodford Clayton, published by Everts & Peck, 1882. Press by J. B. Lippincott & Company, Philadelphia.

Warne Genealogy, by Reverend George Warne Labaw, Pastor of Reformed Church of Preakness, New Jersey, published by Frank Allaban Genealogical Company, 30 W. 42nd Street, New York, 1911.

Where Our History Was Made, by John T. Faris, published by Silver, Burdett & Company, 1923.

Whitman, Walt, Lectures on, by Stephen D. Stephens, Ph.D., Professor of English Literature at Rutgers University, New Brunswick, New Jersey, 1934.

Woolman, John, Journal of, with introduction by John Greenleaf Whittier, published by J. R. Osgood & Company, Boston, 1873.

World Book Encyclopedia, by W. F. Quarrie & Company, Chicago, Ill., 1931. Vols. II, V, VI.

Something in the hazy distance,
Something in the mists of morning,
Loomed and lifted from the water,
Now seemed floating, now seemed flying,
Coming nearer, nearer, nearer.

. . . .

It was neither goose nor diver,
Neither pelican nor heron,
O'er the water floating, flying,
Through the shining mist of morning
But a birch canoe with paddles
Rising sinking on the water,
And within it came a people
From the distant land——.

—HIAWATHA